Also by Arnold B. Kanter
from Catbird Press

The Handbook of Law Firm Mismanagement

ADVANCED LAW FIRM MISMANAGEMENT

From the Offices of
Fairweather, Winters & Sommers

by
ARNOLD B. KANTER

Illustrated by Paul Hoffman

Catbird Press

Text © 1993 Arnold B. Kanter
Illustrations © Paul Hoffman
All rights reserved.

No part of this book may be used or reproduced in any manner without written permission, except in the context of reviews. CATBIRD PRESS, 16 Windsor Road, North Haven, CT 06473. Our books are distributed to the trade by Independent Publishers Group.

Library of Congress Cataloging-in-Publication Data

Kanter, Arnold B., 1942-
Advanced law firm mismanagement : from the offices of Fairweather, Winters & Sommers / by Arnold B. Kanter ; illustrated by Paul Hoffman.
ISBN 0-945774-20-6 (pbk.) : $12.95
1. Lawyers—Humor. I. Title.
PS3561.A477A65 1993
818'.5402—dc 20   92-33557 CIP

For Bernie Nath and Leo Carlin.
Two of the wisest senior partners ever.
Stanley and I are indebted to you
for your teaching and example.

Contents

Introduction 7
Take a Book 10
Otto-matic Dictating 15
Baseballese 20
The Fairweather Hall of Fame 25
The No-Longer-Compliant Client 30
Engagingly Simple 34
Now What Was I Saying? 39
Calling Committees to Order 43
Tailor-made for Law 49
The Best of PALS 53
Shout It from the Highest Desktop 59
In the Long Range . . . 63
Bachelorhood Blues 68
Anything Goes 73
Seasoning Lawyers to Taste 79
Res Ipsa Lunchitor 84
Risk Not, Want Not 89
Pencils Aren't Peanuts 94
Sentimental Slobbery 99
Advice to the Lawlorn 104
If the Moccasin Fits, Wear It 110
Listen, Buddy *or* The Quality of
    Life Is Strained, It Droppeth. . . 115
Playing Lawyer 121
Aiding Legal Aid 125
Have I Got a Firm for You! 130

Ballyhooing the Firm *134*
Oxy and Other Morons *139*
Bar Hopping *144*
Mothers of Invention *150*
Ugly as SIN *155*
Overperfection *160*
Don't Blindly Copy Unless
    You See Why *164*
De-honing Legal Minds *169*
Less Than Super-vision *173*
Safari, So Goody *178*
The Dearly Departed *182*
Managing to Get Along *187*
Have Memo, Will Babble *193*
Retire Early, Avoid the Rush *198*
Il Partnershipio *203*
Crisis *209*
Until Death Do Us Part—Or Longer *213*

Introduction

A week or two ago, six of my partners barged into my office, unannounced. This in itself is not so surprising. Unannounced is the way most people barge. And nobody who comes into my office is announced, anyway.

As it happened, all six bargors were members of the Fairweather, Winters & Sommers Executive Committee. They caught the seventh member of that committee, and its chair, the bargee—me—deep in thought, so much so that I didn't notice them for some time.

"Aha, killick," were my triumphant first words to the group. Actually, they were not exactly addressed to the group, they were more to myself. I'd come up with 28-down, "an anchor formed by a stone enclosed by wood," and was justifiably pleased with myself. When I glanced up and noticed the puzzled looks on the faces of the assembled throng, though, I set aside my crossword and asked in what way I might be of assistance to them.

Perhaps startled by my reference to the anchor, Harry Punctillio sputtered, "Ah, Stanley, aah. . . we'd like you to write things down."

"What the hell're you talking about?" I asked with my customary tact and subtlety.

"About the firm, about your thoughts on the practice of law all these years, your advice, even about you," Harry added. "We want to be able to know all that, pass it on to future generations."

Well, I knew damn well that this was poppycock—a bald-faced attempt to push me out, cut my share of the pie and get rid of me as chairman. And I told them that, in so many words.

But damned if they didn't fool me. And that doesn't happen too often. Nails Nuttree, head of our litigation department, whipped out this piece of paper, signed by all members of the Executive Committee and certified by Stephen Falderall, secretary to the committee, and handed it to me:

Certified Unanimous Resolution

Whereas, the undersigned are duly elected members of the Fairweather, Winters & Sommers Executive Committee; and

Whereas, the Fairweather firm (as it is commonly—though not, strictly speaking, legally correctly—referred to as) has benefited enormously from the legal acumen, wisdom and guidance of its senior partner, to wit, Stanley J. Fairweather (hereinafter referred to as "the aforesaid Stanley J. Fairweather"); and

Whereas, the firm holds the aforesaid Stanley J. Fairweather in deep admiration and respect; and

Whereas, the firm would benefit greatly from the written thoughts and advice of the aforesaid Stanley J. Fairweather; and

Whereas, said thoughts and advice would constitute an important legacy to future generations of lawyers at the firm; and

Whereas, given the suspicious nature of the aforesaid Stanley J. Fairweather, he might be inclined to view this resolution as a bald-faced attempt to push him out of power or cut his share of the pie; and

Whereas, nothing could be further from the truth;

Now, Therefore, Be It Resolved That:

The undersigned unanimously request that the aforesaid Stanley J. Fairweather spend a substantial amount of time writing down his reflections on the practice of law, the firm and his life.

During the pendency of such writing, the aforesaid Stanley J. Fairweather shall remain chair of the Executive Committee and his present percentage draw shall not be reduced.

Important legacy. Deep admiration and respect. So hell, what could I—the aforesaid Stanley J. Fairweather—do? Besides, my secretary, Bertha, thinks it's a good idea.

Take a Book

"**T**ake a book, Bertha." That's how I started this, and how I intend to finish it, too.

You get used to some things. Me, I got used to dictating to a secretary. No, not to a secretary—to Bertha. She's been with me—how long is it now, Bertha? Over forty-three years, she says. She's put up with me all that time. Quite an accomplishment on her part, I'd say.

Anyway, dictation's becoming a lost art. Another decade and it'll be dead altogether. My partners dictate to machines. (I tried it myself a couple of times, in fact, but stopped for two reasons—didn't like it and couldn't figure out how to do it.) Machines, they tell me, are cheaper than people. My *new* partners, they don't even dictate to machines; they type right into these word processors.

Word processors. Maybe because I'm an amateur chef (and a damn good one, too), I always think of a processor as something you throw things into and then watch them come out all done just the way you wanted them—diced, pureed, or whatever. Sometime, soon probably, somebody's going to come up with a *real* word processor. You throw in words, as many as you want, press a button, and out comes whatever you ask for—a contract, a letter, a novel, you name it. Meanwhile, as I watch my partners typing away merrily at their computers, it strikes me as ironic that we've replaced secretaries—because they're too expensive—with lawyers. The wonders of technology.

But no one—much less a machine—could replace Bertha. She is the beginning of most things I do; the middle and end of many, too. You see, I've found that it's

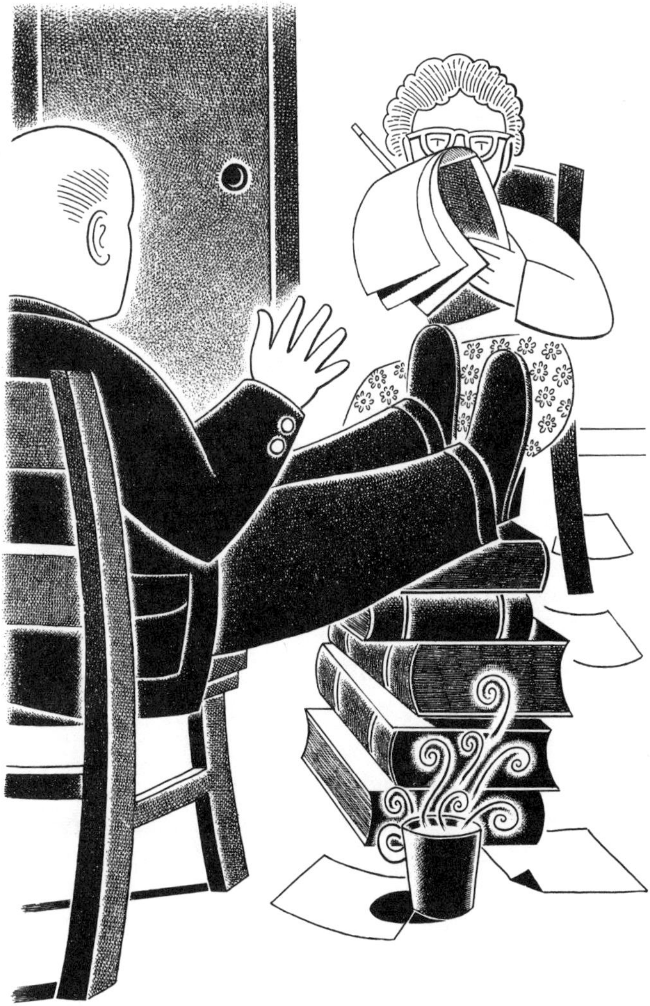

lonely at the top, even at the not-so-lofty top of a law firm. And Bertha's been my constant companion. My advisor. Yes, now that I think of it, my advisor.

It's not that we set aside several hours each week for strategy meetings, Bertha and me. That would be inappropriate. I could never justify that. Hell, who would I bill it to? Can you imagine the entry on my timesheet—three hours: strategy meeting with secretary. No, that would never fly.

But me and Bertha don't need three hours to resolve things, anyway. Only lawyers meeting with other lawyers need three hours to decide anything. My meetings with Bertha generally last in the neighborhood of a minute, two for a long one. Here's how they generally go:

ME (finishing dictating a memo or letter): What do you think, Bertha?

BERTHA: I think it's fine, Mr. Fairweather, but [this means she doesn't think it's fine at all] wouldn't it be better to say [thus and so]?

ME: Maybe you're right, let's try it your way.

Not that I agree with Bertha all of the time. I'd say a good 15 or 20% of the time we do it my way.

Probably closer to 15%.

Which brings me back to dictating. I don't think you can form the kind of relationship Bertha and I have without dictating. Just the two of us, spending all that time in a room together. Her just sitting there, watching me think, then reading my words back to me. You develop a certain rhythm, a tolerance and appreciation for silence. This may seem odd, even perverse, but dictating's a very personal experience (one that, sadly, whole generations of lawyers—and secretaries—are never going to know). And there aren't a whole lot of personal experiences left in law firms today.

Of course, dictating, especially something as long as

a book, has its disadvantages, too. Unless you're a whole lot better dictater than I am, you wind up with a draft. And drafts tend to, well, meander a bit. Of course, I could craft this book the way I craft a contract, or the way Nails Nuttree crafts a brief. Trouble with that, though, is you lose some of the process: how you get to where you got. And I think that process is important in understanding . . . in understanding what? . . . in understanding my life . . . maybe in understanding Life. If you'll pardon my saying so, life's something of a draft. If we're lucky, we may get to polish it up some, correct the grammar and punctuation—spell-check it, perhaps—but we never get it perfect.

I find the same thing's true in my cooking. Take my stew, for example; I call it a "hotchpotch." According to Webster, "hotchpotch" is a thick soup or stew composed of vegetables, potatoes and, usually, meat. It's a heterogeneous mixture whose taste depends upon the quality of its ingredients, how they are put together and what kind of spice one adds. You keep looking for the perfect combination, but you never quite find it.

By the time a fellow approaches eighty—or, let's be honest, runs smack-dab into it—his stew's been simmering quite a while. His broth may be boiling, or foaming over the top; his contents might be a tad soggy. But at least the ingredients are all there, and chances are they've been stirred quite thoroughly. If he's lucky enough, that old fellow may yet hold a pinch or two of spice between his thumb and forefinger to sprinkle around the pot.

So I offer you, my present and future colleagues, this hotchpotch. I'll mix in some of my favorite firm memos, committee meetings and the like to temper my philosophical musings and reminiscences. Take a quick whiff or taste, then eat and make of it what you will. If you find a bit of meat within, chew it well before you swallow. In any case, I hope you find it seasoned to your taste.

You know, I think this is going to be rather fun, inflicting a little wisdom on you people. I thought I'd left philosophy behind in undergraduate school, but I guess I never did. Maybe that's what all managing partners need to be—philosophers. Heaven help us.

Otto-matic Dictating

Now, of course, I'm not the only one at the firm who's had difficulty learning how to use a dictating machine. But this debility created no hardship for me, as I've continued to dictate to Bertha. Others, though, have not been afforded that option. Our Finance Committee mandated first a two-, then a three-lawyers-per-secretary ratio, and instructed all lawyers to learn to use the pocket dictating machines that were distributed to them.

Fortunately, though, our Committee Overseeing Management of Modern Innovative Technology Tending to Ensure Efficiency, the COMMITTEE Committee, scampered to the rescue. They published a concise, 124-page manual entitled "Befriending Your Dictating Machine." The work is copyrighted in the COMMITTEE Committee's name, but I've obtained their permission to reproduce a few of my favorite passages from the manual.

INTRODUCTION

Many lawyers are afraid of their dictating machines. But that's silly. What's that little machine going to do—eat you? No, of course it won't. So start out by relaxing. Lie down. Take a few slow, deep breaths. That's it. Good.

Now think of your dictating machine as your pal. Get to know it, up close and personal, as we say in Olympic years. In fact, many lawyers find it helpful to give their dictating machine a name. Go ahead, don't be embarrassed. After all, your dictating machine is really a sort of pocket secretary—and secretaries have names, don't they? For purposes of this manual, let's call your machine Otto.

Before you begin using Otto, carry him around for awhile. Put him in a pocket, tuck him into a briefcase or purse. Light, isn't he? Sleek, too. Feel how smooth and cool he is. Open him up and close him a couple times. Hear that little click when he's shut good and tight? (Note: use a little discretion as to when and where you play with Otto.)

Now that you're friends, you're ready to learn how Otto works.

HOW YOUR MACHINE WORKS

Your comfort level in using Otto will increase greatly if you understand how Otto works. Actually, it's quite simple.

You'll need just two things to make Otto work: a battery and a teeny-tiny tape.

Think of the battery as Otto's heart, going tick-tick-tick to make him work. (Note: the battery won't actually go tick-tick-tick. That's perfectly normal. Batteries never go tick-tick-tick. Clocks go tick-tick-tick. See our manual entitled "Your Office Clock and How to Use It," copies of which are available in the library.)

The teeny-tiny tape is Otto's brain. It remembers everything you say, and repeats it (but, fortunately, only when you want it to).

Unless you put in both Otto's heart and Otto's brain, Otto won't work. At all. You can dictate and dictate until the cows come home and Otto won't remember a thing you said. And that's not Otto's fault. It's *your* fault.

So it's very important that you give Otto both his heart and his brain. It may help you remember to do this if you think that Otto needs precisely what the tin man and the scarecrow needed when they met Dorothy on her way to Oz. (Note: forget about the lion. Otto doesn't need courage, you do.)

Otto's heart operates differently than your heart or my heart. Otto's heart converts chemical energy into electrical energy by arranging constituent chemicals in such a way that electrons flow from one part (the anode or negative electrode) to another (the cathode or positive electrode) through an external circuit. The voltaic cell is made up of two chemicals (an electrochemical couple) immersed in an electrolyte which produces an oxidation-reduction reaction. The chemical nature of the materials in the electrode determines the voltage. Of course, the current that flows is determined by the total resistance of the circuit or the area of the electrodes. [Stanley's note: at this point the discussion gets a bit technical for us former philosophy majors, delving as it does into ionic conductivity and lapsing finally into the history of the battery and its founder, Alessandro Volta, a professor of natural philosophy at PU (the University of Pavia in Italy). I omit here entirely the discussion of Otto's brain, written by my partner Percifal Snikkety, whose moral and physiological aversion to cutting up frogs deprived the world of a fine physician.]

TIPS ON USING YOUR DICTATING MACHINE

Now that you understand how Otto works, you're ready to begin the adventure of dictating. Rather than come up with a boring abstract list of do's and don'ts, we've contacted some of the firm's premier dicaters and asked them for their insights and tips, which are set forth below:

1. Before beginning to dictate, test to make sure your machine is working. I once forgot to do that and found, after dictating a forty-two page brief, that all I had on the tape was my daughter, Felicia, singing "Twinkle, Twinkle, Little Star." While it was a rather good rendition, I knew that the Court of Appeals would prefer more direct authority in support of my client's position. To test your machine, try dictating something into it, such as "Testing one, two,

eight," and playing it back. Do not use "Testing one, two, three." Everybody uses that, so when you play it back you will not know whether the machine is actually working or whether you are hearing somebody else's test (since you won't recognize your own voice on the machine). (Stephen I. Falderall)

2. Get to know the buttons on your machine. There's one on the top that you have to press down in order to record. No, maybe it's on the side. If you push something up you can fast forward or down you can fast backward. But if you push the wrong button (which is either on the side or the top) along with something else, it will erase everything. So be very careful. (Alphonse Proust)

3. When dictating, it will be helpful to your secretary if you spell out proper names and difficult or confusing words, and indicate the punctuation. Do not, however, insult your secretary in the process. For example:

Correct

"Please take a letter to Joseph Pocaccioni, P-O-C-A-C-C-I-O-N-I. Dear Joe, colon, Thanks for yours of the 19th, comma, which arrived yesterday. Paragraph. Notwithstanding your argument that your client should be made whole, W-H-O-L-E, comma, I believe that this cannot be sustained because he was in pari delicto, I-N P-A-R-I D-E-L-I-C-T-O, underlined."

Incorrect

"Please take, T-A-K-E, a letter to Joseph Pocaccioni. Dear Joe, J-O-E, colon, Thanks for yours of the 19th, comma, C-O-M-M-A, which arrived yesterday. (The letter, not the comma). Paragraph. Notwithstanding your argument that, no comma, your client should be made whole, I believe that this cannot be sustained because he was in pari delicto (I'm not sure how the hell you spell that, look it up.)"

Also, when indicating the punctuation, do not pretend that you are Victor Borge. (Seymour I. Plain)

4. Before you dictate, think. Organize your thoughts. Failure to do this may lead to your repeating yourself. Once you have said something once, you don't need to say it over again another way. To say things over and over again wastes a lot of time. Also, it is annoying to have to read something that is said over and over again. In short, avoid saying things over and over again at all costs. Thinking is also permitted after you begin dictating. (Jane Hokum-Cohen)

5. Before erasing a tape that you receive from somebody else, you may want to listen to it. You'd be surprised what sort of wild and lurid things you can find on used tapes. For a list of whose tapes you're likely to hear the best stuff on, contact the office manager. (Anonymous)

[STANLEY'S NOTE: The long hours invested by COMMITTEE Committee members in writing "Befriending Your Dictating Machine" were rewarded when the publication was awarded the 1989 Fairweather Prize for Literature. Movie rights have been optioned to Warner Brothers, which is reportedly negotiating with Dustin Hoffman to play the role of Otto.]

Baseballese

Would I do it all over again? People ask me that all the time these days. I guess that's a sign of age, being asked if you'd do it over again.

There may be dumber questions. But not too many.

We don't get the option to do it all over again. Unless, that is, you're one of them that believe you'll come back as a llama in the next life. Me, I don't believe it. But if I did, I wouldn't worry about it now. I'd worry about it in the next life, by which time I would hope llamas might have achieved a somewhat loftier position than they've managed so far.

I guess I'm not big on hypotheticals. At least not the type that aren't related to the here and now. I've got nothing against philosophy, mind you. In fact, I majored in philosophy. But I'm not the type to spend a lot of time contemplating abstract questions, like whether God exists. I prefer a philosophy borne of experience. I'm more your practical philosopher type. So, if I did spend time thinking about God, I'd be interested in things that really matter—like, if God were a pitcher, would he be a righty or a southpaw?

Maybe folks who ask me about doing it all over again mean to ask whether there's anything I'd do differently. Show me the person who answers "no" to that question and I'll show you one arrogant dude.

Law's been good to me. Real good. But that doesn't mean I wouldn't rather have been a shortstop for the Chicago Cubs. Fellow would have to be nuts to think otherwise.

Advanced Law Firm Mismanagement

I was born a Cubs fan. And I suppose that explains a lot about me. Takes character, being a Cubs fan. And patience. And faith. And perspective. And many other things, too.

Take 1969, for example. We're leading the league by ten games in September. Coasting along. Pennant's in the bag. So I figure it's safe to leave the country, take a vacation to Mexico, the Yucatan. Besides, I've just closed a public offering of convertible preferred for a major client. Perfect timing.

And what do the Cubs do? Blow it. But wait, it's worse than that. Who do they blow it to? Not the Dodgers, or the Giants. No, the Mets. They lose it to the damn Mets. The only Spanish I could read in the newspapers around Chichenitza were the headlines in the sports section each day: "Los Mets Ganan." Talk about suffering. Talk about humiliation. The Mets.

Fortunately, I'm over that 1969 disappointment now. I don't think of it more than two or three times a week, during the winter months. More, of course, during the season.

Baseball's a lawyer's game. Loaded down with rules. You've got to appreciate the fine points to love baseball. And you've got to accept its pace, too. Investment bankers hate baseball, I'll bet. Too slow for them. And not enough heads get knocked.

Yes, shortstop for the Chicago Cubs, that's about the pinnacle to which man can aspire. There are more glorious positions. Pitcher, I suppose. But I'd like to be out there every day, not just once or twice a week. Others might prefer to be the slugger who belts forty home runs and bats in a hundred and twenty. But as for me, I'd rather turn a double play, or throw someone out from the hole or slap a tag on a runner trying to swipe second. (Maybe that's the definition of maturity—the point at which you'd rather see a smooth double play than a long home run.)

You may think I'm veering pretty far from the law, talking about baseball. But I don't think so, really. Law firms today have gone the way of baseball teams, I'm afraid. Used to be, you could count on seeing the same players out there from season to season. Now, of course, ballplayers go to the highest bidder—free agents. Damn expensive free agents, if you ask me.

And it's getting so that law firms don't look the same from year to year, either. Partners display just about the same loyalty to their firms as ballplayers do to their teams. Actually, it's worse than that. Baseball teams, at least, sign players to multi-year contracts. Partners take off midseason for an opportunity to make some more money at another firm (and take part of the team along with them). They see their careers as short, like athletes. If they're in a hot specialty—say environmental law, at the moment—and they see greener pastures elsewhere, they figure they'd better move there. There's no telling how long the specialty will stay hot. After all, what are all the antitrust and mergers-and-acquisitions lawyers doing today?

I don't blame individual partners for the popularity of free agency. I blame us law firms. Our failures have made it possible. We've tried to overcome those failures with partnership agreements that provide huge economic disincentives for leaving the firm. But they haven't worked. The courts won't enforce them. And our failures are not primarily economic, anyway. The thought that dollars are holding law firms together is mortifying.

Whomever's to blame, though, the implications of partner free agency are manifold. What do you tell the law student who has been romanced by the firm's hiring partner and serenaded with the firm's anthem, when the student arrives to find out that the hiring partner has moved crosstown to a firm whose offer the student declined? Do you really want to spend a hundred thousand bucks on a glossy firm brochure that features the photo of a partner who may be gone before the four colors of ink are dry? And are you prepared to tout the virtues of a partner in another practice area to one of your valued clients, when that partner may leave the firm and take the client with him?

Let's look for the bright side, though. I've been thinking that there ought to be room for somebody creative to turn a buck off of all this lawyer mobility. I've always longed to have my picture on one of those baseball cards that kids trade with one another. Maybe we ought to package partner trading cards. Photo of the partner on the front in his or her work uniform. And on the back, the vital statistics—practice area, billings, hours worked and earnings. I'll bet a rookie Stanley J. Fairweather partner card, in mint condition, would fetch a pretty penny, even without the bubble gum.

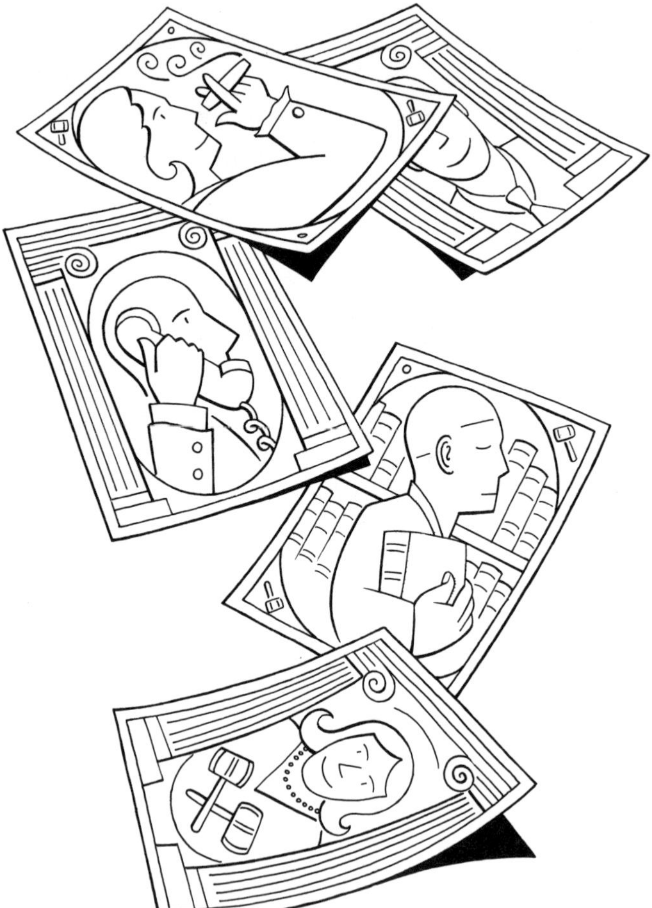

The Fairweather Hall of Fame

My days of participating in sports are over, but sports continues to play an important role for lawyers at Fairweather, Winters & Sommers. Vance "Rip" Winkle III, who lettered twice in cribbage at Princeton and was named second team, all-Ivy, in his senior year, chairs the Committee on Health in Practice (CHIP). CHIP's jurisdiction extends to a broad range of subjects that affect the health and fitness of the FWS family. But among all of CHIP'S responsibilities, none weighs more heavily on its members than elevating attorneys to the FWS Hall of Fame.

Though less celebrated than the Baseball Hall of Fame in Cooperstown or the Football Hall of Fame in Canton, the FWS Hall of Fame is revered by a small but influential core of lawyer/sports buffs from coast to coast. In a typical year, the FWS Hall attracts over twelve visitors, mainly family of those there enshrined. The FWS Hall is housed in a conference room on the 55th floor, which is dedicated exclusively to that purpose, except when a major Nails Nuttree litigation matter occupies the conference room for eight months running and forces the temporary relocation of the Hall to a supply closet on the 54th floor.

For its first twenty years, under the Hall's charter, election was restricted to those who "brought glory on the Fairweather firm name through excelling on one of the firm teams that participate in the lawyer sports leagues." Unfortunately, in those two decades nobody was elected to membership in the Hall. Some attributed this to the abysmal showing of the firm's lawyer league teams. Others pointed to the requirement of unanimous CHIP approval for election, noting that Nails had voted "nay" on every candidate presented. While Nails was prepared to defend each of his votes on the merits—and at considerable length—some partners suspected that it was his reluctance to move the files of his latest antitrust case out of the Hall conference room that accounted for more than a few of Nails' votes.

Some fifteen years ago, however, the standard for election to the FWS Hall was amended in two important respects. Those elected no longer needed to "bring glory" through "excelling," but rather needed only "not unduly sully the Fairweather firm name" through "trying his darndest." And, more importantly, a candidate needed to receive only majority support of CHIP. Under these new rules, twenty-seven lawyers have been inducted, including those immortalized by the plaques below:

REX A. GLADHAND

Rex Gladhand, member of the trusts & estates department, specialist in codicils and second baseman on the FWS softball team, 1964-79. Rex was noted for his good glove, a Rawlings Nellie Fox model with a deep reddish brown hue.

Rex oiled his glove each game day, and it may be this oiling fetish that was responsible for the many errors in which the ball slipped out of his hand as he was throwing to first. Though his lifetime batting average was only .212, Rex was known as "Mr. Clutch" to many partners on the team (and Mr. Gladhand to the associates on the team). His bunt single in the eighth inning of the 1973 playoff game led to the run that averted a 23-0 shutout in the team's heart-breaking 23-1 loss to Fretch & Swill. Rex is probably best known, though, for the hidden ball trick that he attempted on Stinky Jermens of Skiddem, Harps. Jermens was on second base in a tie game, when Rex approached the mound to suggest to the FWS pitcher, Hiram Miltoast, that Stinky might fall for the old hidden ball trick, if it were done cleverly. By "done cleverly" Rex indicated that the ball would have to be hidden someplace other than in his glove, where Stinky would be sure to notice it. As the rest of the infield circled the mound, Rex slipped the ball down the rear of his left pantsleg, then resumed his position at second base. As Stinky took his leadoff, Rex shouted "I've got the ball," but before he could retrieve it from his pantsleg, Stinky had circled the bases with the winning run.

SHELDON I. HORVITZ

Sheldon I. Horvitz, member of the real estate department, specialist in enfoefments, and sixth man on the FWS basketball team, 1972-79. Last of the great two-handed set shooters, Sheldon came off the bench often to spark the FWS Torts to near-victories in several not-very-important games. Sheldon tended to telegraph his set shot somewhat by requiring his four teammates to form a box around him so that he could get the shot off. This hampered the team's ability to rebound or defend against the fast break on missed shots. Sheldon was perhaps best known, though, for his commitment to freedom of religion in basketball. Noting that members of the Christian faith sometimes crossed themselves prior to shooting free throws, Sheldon, an Orthodox Jew, initiated the practice of davening at the line before shooting free throws. This tended to disrupt the game somewhat, as it required a minyan of ten players. When an opposing team objected, however, Sheldon took the matter to court and won. His law review article on the topic, "Davening at Basketball Games: Free Exercise at the Free Throw Line," won wide praise among academic constitutional lawyers and netted him the honor of 1976 B'nai Brith Athlete of the Year.

Some five years ago, a new era dawned in the FWS Hall of Fame. The impetus for that era was a petition by an ad hoc group that called itself CATCH, the Committee Against the Closed Hall. The petition began as follows:

> We the undersigned protest vigorously against the policies of CHIP that have led to population of the FWS Hall of Fame exclusively by sports-oriented types. If we'd have wanted to play sports, we'd have done it professionally. Instead, we've chosen to become lawyers and to demonstrate our athleticism through our lawyerly activities. We decry the fact that this lawyerly athleticism has been scorned by CHIP in choosing members of the FWS Hall.

After four years of trying to figure out what CATCH meant by "lawyerly athleticism," the first lawlete, as members of that group have come to be called, was inducted this year. Godfrey Bleschieu's plaque reads as follows:

GODFREY A. BLESCHIEU

Godfrey A. Bleschieu, member of the corporate department, specialist in long, boring, repetitive documentation. At 11:23 P.M. on Friday, November 14, 1991, Godfrey completed proofreading the thirty-fourth and final draft of a 96-page collateral loan agreement and carried the original up three flights of stairs, taken two stairs at a time, to the duplicating department, only to find that the entire duplicating department had retired for the night. As the document absolutely, positively had to be delivered to the offices of the client by 4 A.M. on the 15th—since November has thirty days and the fifteenth is the midpoint, and 4 A.M. is the client's favorite time—Godfrey pressed into action, photocopying the necessary forty-two copies of the agreement himself. He used the automatic stapling feature of the photocopying machine. By 12:47 this process had been completed, but, checking the copies, Godfrey discovered that the machine had automatically stapled sixteen of the pages in the wrong order. Due to cost considerations, Godfrey did not recopy the document, but commenced to unstaple the agreements by hand and rearrange the pages. In so doing, Godfrey sustained twenty-three claw punctures and one hundred and six paper cuts, despite being very careful. Taking pains not to bleed on the pages, he then restapled the documents by hand and put them, three at a time, into fourteen large, expandable envelopes. By now it was 3:20 A.M., plenty of time to take a taxi across town to the client's office. As luck would have it, though, no taxi was available, so Godfrey had to run the fourteen large envelopes the two miles to the client's office. He arrived at 3:58 A.M. and left the documents outside the client's door, where the client picked them up on Monday the 17th, around 9 or 10 A.M.

The induction of Godfrey into the Hall raised the hopes of all lawletes that their accomplishments, too, would at last receive the recognition they deserved. This hope will be put to the test next year, when CHIP considers whether Harriet Akers' document production prowess (she recently bench-pressed a two-hundred-pound box of forty-year-old accounts receivable ledgers) merits elevation to the Hall.

The No-Longer-Compliant Client

I'd like to say a word or two here about the attorney-client privilege. No, I don't mean about some arcane rules governing what may or may not be introduced into evidence. I mean about the privilege of an attorney representing a client.

I hear lawyers bemoan the fact that clients no longer have any loyalty to law firms. I guess I've bemoaned that a time or two myself, come to think of it. But loyalty's a two-way street: traffic's got to run both ways.

Maybe a very short history of my attorney-client relationships would be in order. Back when I came out of law school in nineteen hundred and thirty-seven, your client was your best friend. Not all of them were, of course, but many.

Clients didn't call me so much to learn the law (though every once in a while I'd tell them about that, too). They called me for my advice. Period. The advice might be about the law. Or it might be about their business. But it might just as well be about their golf game, or their son or daughter, or most anything else. I'll bet I'm "Uncle Stanley" to about sixty or so clients' kids, scattered from coast to coast. (A bunch of those "kids" are pretty substantial clients themselves, by the way.)

That type of relationship made a lawyer feel pretty darn good. You were a counselor, a trusted friend, a confidant. You didn't feel like a hired gunslinger, paid by the bullet—even if that's what you were.

And you, in turn, treated your client with respect. His problems mattered to you. He was a real human being, not a client code number that you billed quarter-hours for five-minute phone calls.

The result seemed to be a happy one for both parties. Your client had a lawyer for life. And you had a client for life. Not that it ever was expressed that way. It didn't have to be. Nothing else would have occurred to either of you.

Then something changed. That much is for sure. But it's difficult figuring out exactly how and why the attorney-client privilege became the attorney-client burden. I can't pinpoint the answer, but I've got some notion of what it had to do with.

One thing it had to do with is size. Size of clients and size of law firms. The bigger they both got, the tougher it became for the bond between attorney and client to form. Inside both the client and the law firm, the individual identified less with the organization. This happened, in part, because mentor relationships began to disappear. And the disappearance of those mentor relationships within both organizations had an important impact upon attorney-client relationships, because it was those mentors who knew firsthand and taught younger people at both the client and the law firm how to relate to one another. Used to be, I worked with my young associates all the time. Truth is, I can't remember the last time I worked with an associate.

Another thing the change had to do with is greed. Greed with a short-term focus. As we law firms focused more and more on our bottom lines, the emphasis shifted from counseling clients and solving their problems, to maximizing the fees the firm would receive from the client—that year. That revised focus had a big impact on the relationship between lawyers and clients. It put the client second, not first.

And a final thing the change had to do with—though both my granddaughter, Maggie, and my friend and partner, FWS-Hall-of-Famer Sheldon Horvitz, would be distressed to hear me say so—was the success of the law as an instrument of social policy. When law became seen as the answer to societal ills, law schools attracted students who weren't so much interested in clients as they were in causes. Those students never realized that the case names in their law school casebooks were real people. They viewed the client as a means of getting at challenging intellectual issues that interested them. Clients, in other words, were there to serve lawyers' interests, not the other way around. Too many lawyers, I'm afraid, began to look down on clients as a necessary evil, a burden.

For many blissful years—some of my partners would say the golden years of our practice—clients seemed content to allow us lawyers to conduct a cost-plus business, unsullied by anything so clearly beneath a profession's dignity as competition. They sent all of their legal business to a single firm and continued to pay five- and six-figure statements "for legal services rendered on the XYZ matter" without questioning what services were rendered, whether they were necessary or whether they were worth the fee.

But then, one day, some client somewhere ate of the tree of knowledge—and ruined everything. He (or she, but probably he) awoke one day and exclaimed to himself, "Wait a minute, *I'm* the damn client. Who says I have to take all of my work to one firm? Who says I can't negotiate the fees that I'll be charged? Who says I can't demand information about the time and expenses incurred on my behalf?" (Quite likely, the person asking these questions was one of our former associates, passed over for partnership because we didn't think he was good enough, who then went to work as general counsel for a large corporate client. Talk about spoil sports.)

In any case, when the dust had settled we were left with something like this: before being retained by a client, a law firm was required to make a presentation of its qualifications (compete in a beauty contest, as it became known). Prior to the decision to hire a firm, the client and firm engaged in a lengthy discussion enumerating what the fees and expenses would be. This resulted in what came to be called an engagement letter (I think I'd call it a prenuptial agreement). Finally, when services were billed, the client requested and received excruciating detail as to time and expenses. And if the client was not satisfied with the statement, it might elect to call in an independent auditor to review the charges.

So, it seems that attorneys and clients have moved from best friends to adversaries. Now, of course, some may see a sunny side to all of this. After all, if clients and attorneys are adversaries, clients are going to need somebody to represent them in negotiating their relationships with their own attorneys. Now *there's* a specialty of the future for you. Or for somebody. But not for me. Personally, I'm still counting my clients as valued friends. At my age, perhaps I could afford to lose a client if I had to, but not a friend.

Engagingly Simple

Now, once our firm realized that clients were requiring written agreements with their law firms, our Committee on Firm Forms (COFF) lost precious little time in coming up with a form engagement letter. This letter has gained narrow-spread acceptance among our clients.

FORM ENGAGEMENT LETTER

Dear   :

Nice to see you/talk to you/visit with you/sorry I missed you [please select only one] the other day. I'm so glad that we were able to reach agreement so easily and I certainly look forward to our working together on this matter. To avoid any little misunderstandings that might otherwise pop up down the road, we both thought that we should reduce our agreement to writing. Rather than come up with a big, formal-looking contract, I thought we'd use this simple little letter.

Definition of Terms

As used in this agreement, the following terms shall have the meanings ascribed to them below, to wit:

"You" shall mean the XYZ Corporation, any wholly- or majority-owned subsidiary thereof, any successor thereto by merger, consolidation, assignment or otherwise, any officer or director thereof, and generally anybody else who might possibly be considered a you, it being intended that the word "you" be construed as broadly as humanly and legally possible.

"We" shall mean the Fairweather, Winters & Sommers law firm, defined so as to maximize said firm's rights and to limit said firm's liabilities.

"Us" shall mean You and We.

"Them" shall mean everybody except Us.

Scope of Representation

We shall represent You in the Whole Deal. "Whole Deal" means everything to do with the acquisition of ABC Corporation, from Soup to Nuts. "Soup" means the investigation, negotiation and drafting of the agreement to acquire ABC. "Nuts" means the closing or blow-up and litigation of the Whole Deal. In the unlikely event that the acquisition is consummated, the "Whole Deal" shall include everything up to and including the ultimate, final and irreversible demise of ABC. While this definition may seem overly broad, the complex way in which we will document the transaction will require that You retain We forever to help You try to understand what happened to You.

Professional Handling/Lack of Conflict

We undertake to represent You in a professional manner to the best of our somewhat limited ability, and to leave no stone unturned (or unbilled for). We will try our darndest to avoid serious conflicts of interest or at least to build an Asian Wall around somebody, if that will help.

Staffing

We take particular pride in assigning the right level of attorney to perform each task in the Whole Deal. Thus, for example, we use great care not to assign work to a busy partner that could be performed adequately by an idle associate. Notwithstanding the foregoing, when work is a little slow at the firm, it may become necessary that our most senior (and expensive) partners perform tasks that at many other firms are delegated unwisely to associates or paralegals. That's part of the tradition We have established over the years which has made our firm what it is today.

Fee Estimate

You have asked We to estimate the fees that may be involved in the Whole Deal. We have informed You that this is impossible. You have informed We that that's no excuse and You want a fee estimate. Subject to the following caveats, then, it is our estimate that the fees for the Whole Deal will be in the general neighborhood of "quite-a-bit-but-not-too-much-considering-what's-involved." In arriving at the foregoing estimate, we have assumed that:

1. Them will be extremely accommodating and will accept our form purchase agreement without change.
2. You will do your part quickly and timely, and will not make unreasonable demands upon We.
3. Nothing tricky will turn up.
4. No force majeur or force mineur will screw things up.

You acknowledge that this fee estimate is inherently improbable, unreliable and unenforceable. You agree to pay We fees calculated as provided below, even though such fees will most likely turn out to range between "way-too-much" and "you've-got-to-be-kidding."

Calculation of Fees

In general, We will bill You on an hourly basis. Our lawyers, paralegals and librarians will keep track of the amount of time they spend on the Whole Deal by noting each quarter hour of their work. They will be reminded to do this by the bell that sounds four times per hour throughout our office. This time will be entered into a computer that contains each person's hourly rate. You will not be informed of those hourly rates since they are top secret and none of your business, anyway. Even if We did inform You of the hourly rates, however, they would not be of much use, since We change the hourly rates at time intervals best described as "whenever We feel like it."

We may deviate from the hourly rate to charge You a premium if the result We achieve is better than We expected. Since We tend to be very conservative and pessimistic in our expectations, You should expect that our results will be better than We expected more often than You expect. The results may be better than We expected even when We lose, since We may lose by less than We expected. This deserves a premium. The amount of the premium plus the hourly fees shall not exceed "grossly-outrageous." We'll determine that.

Billings

To make sure that We get paid, You will give We a retainer. This retainer is not because We don't trust You, but because We'll feel more comfortable that way and that's the way We always do it. In addition to the retainer, You will pay We each month the amount of our hourly billing, plus our expenses, by return mail. If You do not pay these bills promptly, We may do any or all of the following:

    a. cease working on the Whole Deal;
    b. add interest to our bill at or above the highest rate provided by law;
    c. put our firm administrator, Lt. Colonel Clinton Hargraves, CPA, on the matter;
    d. refer the matter to our Billing Committee; or
    e. sue your rear end.

Expenses

In incurring expenses, We shall live in the manner to which We would like to become accustomed, and adhere to the standard of the reasonably frugal billionaire. When We are working on the Whole Deal, We will not go out to dinner at expensive restaurants. Instead, to save time, We will order dinner in from those restaurants and bill You for our eating time, as well as for the food. We will fly first class to avoid the risk that someone sitting next to We in the cramped coach seating might see some of the ultra-confidential documents that We are preparing for You (or read our ultra-confidential novel). Finally, We have discovered that, on out-of-town trips, it is more efficient in the long run for You to have We taken everywhere by a chauffeured limousine that will wait downstairs until the meeting is over. This saves money on delivery costs, since the limo driver can go to whatever five-star restaurant We have ordered lunch from to pick it up. If You want to quibble about expenses, You may do so, but frankly, We find that distasteful.

Audit

If You are dissatisfied with any bill, You may choose to call for an audit by any certified public accountant You choose, provided that such public accountant is satisfactory to We. The only public accountant satisfactory to We is Clinton Hargraves, Jr., CPA ("Little Clint"). If Little Clint finds that we have ripped you off unconscionably, we'll reduce the bill by knocking a little off. Otherwise, You will pay our bill, plus all of Little Clint's fees.

We trust that this letter will meet with your complete approval and that You will indicate that approval by signing a copy of this letter. Hope this little note finds you and your family well.

Sincerely,

Sounds Pretty
Good to Us

Now What Was I Saying?

"Stanley, what got you interested in the law?" people always ask me. Naw, people don't always ask me that. In fact, they never do. But I thought that might make a nice, subtle transition into the topic.

Maybe I should give up on subtle transitions. I've never been long on subtlety. That may be a weakness of mine. But I believe in telling a person what I think. Some think it's not tactful. Some regard it as cruel. But I disagree.

Let's consider a couple examples. Take the young lawyer at our firm who has got some good tools, but isn't measuring up to what you want. Our tendency is to beat around the bush and hope things will change, rather than sit down with him, tell him what's wrong and what needs to be done to fix it. We think we're being kind to the fellow by not being too critical. I did that myself a number of times, when I was younger.

Know what happens down the road, though, in my experience? The problem doesn't just fix itself. It gets worse. So, years later you're left with having to tell the lawyer that he'd better look for a new place to work. All of this comes as a big shock to him. You've missed an opportunity for him to address the problem. And you've left him feeling bad about you and the firm. So I've found that a little forthrightness early on is a lot less painful for all concerned, in the long run.

So to avoid being taken in by people who are too kind in their evaluations, I've developed five principles for evaluating associate evaluations. Here they are:

1. All associates rated lousy are lousy, unless the evaluation is based on the comments of Nails Nuttree or a few other partners who are impossible to work with. Tell these associates to leave within three months. Help them in any way you can. They may hate you now, but many of them will thank you later. Move "Nailed" associates to more hospitable surroundings and give them a chance to succeed.

2. Sub-par and average associates in under-staffed departments are probably lousy, but are being protected because the department needs the bodies.

3. Average associates in other departments, who have been with the firm at least three years, will not become partners.

4. Associates whose hours are low relative to other associates in a department generally are weak associates. The marketplace is working in not generating the same level of assignments for them as for others in the department.

5. To evaluate the quality of above-average or star performers, evaluate the evaluators.

Let's take one other example of telling it like it is. Several years ago, I was negotiating a contract to buy a corporation that was represented by a partner at another prominent Chicago law firm—we'll call him Henry Jansing, because that's his name.

Henry knew that some of his client's receivables were just plain uncollectable. The situation was a bit complicated, but let's say that Henry, in deciding not to reveal this information, was not being fraudulent, but was less than forthcoming or candid—far less. Maybe he thought he could slip one by an old septuagenarian. Eventually, though, I asked the right question, discovered the right document, and the facts came to light. Naturally, I began to wonder whether anything that Henry had said during the entire negotiation was trustworthy. And that doubt has continued to haunt Henry in every negotiation he has since had with me and with any of the many partners I've told the story to.

What am I saying here—that honesty's the best policy? Bluntness is better than subtlety? Maybe. But I think it's more than that. There seems to be a premium paid for cleverness these days. You take what you can get away with. You keep people guessing. You never show your cards. You assume that the other guy's your adversary, that what he gets diminishes what's left for you. I see that attitude wherever I look today, in law and in life.

That's not the style I prefer, though. I like to know where a person stands. And that that person will still be standing there even if I look away for a minute. It may be hopelessly romantic of me to think so (though hopeless romanticism is not something I'm frequently accused of), but I believe that there used to be a lot more of that type of reliability than there is today. I'm not sure what's to blame for it, but I think we've curtailed our natural instinct to say what we think and to do what we say. It would be nice to recapture some of those instincts.

. . . and so that's how I got interested in law. No, that doesn't make sense, does it. Seems I've gotten off on a bit of a tangent. But I'm not going to apologize for that. In fact, I think we need more tangents.

You may think that I have come to this point of view in my advanced years only because I'm not able to stick to a subject anymore. Not true. I've always been pro-tangent.

You see, I think that we lawyers are altogether too lineal. We approach things logically, try to get from point A to point B. We expend all of our creativity trying to avoid detours on the road. Anything that gets in the way we cast aside; any scenic turnoff we drive right past. That approach may sometimes lead to a good, workmanlike result. But it often doesn't lead to the kind of creativity that's necessary in the law today. That creativity demands an open mind, a willingness sometimes to travel down a few wrong paths, a sense of humor. (By the way, did you know that a tangent is a small upright flat-ended metal pin at the inner end of a clavichord key which strikes the string and produces a tone? Tuck it away, never can tell when that knowledge may come in handy.)

And even if the tangent you take doesn't lead anywhere, the detour should add a little fun to your practice. Fun. Now there's a word you don't hear much anymore linked to the practice of law. It's almost as if the two were inconsistent. Law's a serious business these days. So if you're having fun, there must be something wrong.

I don't believe that for a minute. Soon as I stop having fun at this, I'm out of here. I'll try something else. Too late to play shortstop for the Cubs, I guess, but I'll bet I could still manage those buggers to a World Series.

Calling Committees to Order

Some of my partners do not share my belief that tangents are healthy. Indeed, we seem constantly to strive for more rules and more order. For example, several years ago some of my partners became so alarmed at the amount of time wasted at our firm committee meetings that they instituted a successful drive to amend the firm's Handbook on Committee Meetings. The amendment effort itself consumed more than two years, due largely to a jurisdictional dispute between the Committee on Handbooks and the Committee on Committees, and a lengthy filibuster by Sheldon Horvitz at the partnership meeting that adopted the amendment. Horvitz saw the rule change requiring debate to be on point as directed personally at him, and agreed to end his filibuster only when his right to make irrelevant political points was, as he put it, "grandparented in." Despite the large amount of time devoted to the amendment, most of those who attended the party celebrating adoption of the new rules agreed that the final result (reproduced below) made the effort well worth the candle.

COMMITTEES
 1.1 <u>Definition</u>. A committee is a group of two or more persons charged with considering an issue or a related series of issues in enormous detail, at great length and without discernible benefit to the firm.
 1.2 <u>Persons</u>. Persons shall mean partners in the firm

or, in exceptional situations and on particularly insignificant committees, associates.

1.3 <u>Committee Name</u>. Each committee shall be given a name which conveys some sense of what the committee is considering, assuming, *arguendo*, that the committee is considering what it is charged with considering. Where possible, the committee name shall form an acronym.

1.4 <u>Number of Members</u>. No committee shall have more than seven members. Notwithstanding the foregoing, any committee may have more than seven members if the Executive Committee deems it politic.

1.5 <u>Types of Members</u>. Committee members may be officio, ex officio or non officio.

1.6 <u>Officio Members</u>. An officio member shall be expected to attend meetings and shall be entitled to one vote on each matter to come before the committee. In exceptional situations, a committee may determine to give each officio member two votes.

1.7 <u>Ex Officio Members</u>. An ex officio member shall be a former officio member. An ex officio member need not attend meetings and shall have no vote. An ex officio member shall decide which votes of officio members to count.

1.8 <u>Non Officio Members</u>. Secretaries of ex officio members shall be non officio members. Non officio members shall be the only ones who know what's going on.

1.9 <u>Appointment</u>. Committee members shall be appointed by the Executive Committee, with the advice and consent of Stanley J. Fairweather. Advice and consent means that if Stanley advises, the Executive Committee consents.

1.10 <u>Whom to Appoint</u>. No more than one significant partner shall be appointed to a committee other than the Executive Committee. Only extremely unproductive partners may serve on more than one committee. Membership on committees shall be distributed proportionately among the firm's departments so as not to ruffle feathers.

1.11 Term. Committee members shall serve at the pleasure of the Executive Committee. The Executive Committee is pleased when members of other committees vote the way the Executive Committee wants them to vote.

1.12 Types of Committees. Committees may be standing or ad hoc.

1.13 Standing Committees. Standing committees shall be committees that are expected to last a long time. Standing committee members may, nonetheless, sit at meetings.

1.14 Ad Hoc Committees. Ad hoc committees shall be committees that are expected to be of limited duration, but in fact shall last forever. Ad hoc committees shall vote in Latin.

TRANSACTION OF COMMITTEE BUSINESS

2.1 Frequency of Meetings. Meetings shall be held whenever there is business to transact or when it shall strike the chair that it's been an awfully long time since the committee last met.

2.2 Notice. Notice of a meeting shall be given at least fifteen minutes before the meeting is to commence. Notice may be given by memo, by voice mail or by stopping by a committee member's office. If notice is given more than thirty minutes prior to a meeting, a reminder notice shall be given.

2.3 Quorum. A quorum shall consist of whoever shows up, unless somebody wishes to question a quorum. If somebody wishes to question a quorum, that person shall look for a quorum to question. If nobody shows up, the meeting shall be short.

2.4 Length of Meetings. Meetings shall be limited to one-and-a-half hours, unless something's really important.

Something's really important if the meeting lasts more than one-and-a-half hours.

2.5 <u>Small Talk</u>. Meetings shall begin with a limited amount of small talk, provided, however, that small talk shall not deteriorate into jokes regarding sex organ size. If it does so deteriorate, committee members (after laughing) shall agree unanimously that the joke was in extremely poor taste and does not reflect the policy of the firm.

2.6 <u>Call to Order</u>. After the small talk, the chair shall call the meeting to order by announcing, "Okay, let's knock it off."

2.7 <u>Chair</u>. The chair shall be selected by the Executive Committee. Co-chairs shall be selected if it's too tough to pick one chair, or if the person chosen as chair has an identical twin in the firm.

2.8 <u>Substitute Chair</u>. In the absence of the chair or co-chair, the meeting shall be chaired by the first to tire of small talk.

2.9 <u>Minutes</u>. The chair may appoint a secretary to take minutes of the meeting. Minutes of committee meetings shall be available for inspection by all lawyers at the firm, unless those minutes would tend to subject the committee or other lawyers at the firm to ridicule. Very few committee minutes shall be available for inspection.

2.10 <u>Lunch</u>. Committee members may elect to bring their own lunch in a brown bag or in a lunch pail with a Disney character on it, or to order out to the Mahzel Deli. The Mahzel Deli bill shall be allocated among committee members ordering out, in proportion to the weight of the committee member. Committee members may trade portions of their lunch with other committee members so long as such trades are fair and do not unduly interfere with the transaction of other business at the meeting.

2.11 <u>Business at Lunch</u>. The committee shall transact

business while lunch is being eaten, provided, however, that nobody shall talk with his mouth full.

2.12 Jurisdiction. If there is a question as to whether the matter being discussed is within the jurisdiction of the committee, that matter shall be referred to the Committee on Committees. If there shall be a question as to whether the Committee on Committees has jurisdiction, the matter shall be referred to the Executive Committee. If there's still doubt, Stanley will decide.

2.13 On Point. Discussion shall at all times after the initial small talk remain on point. The chair shall decide whether discussion is on point. Notwithstanding the foregoing, Sheldon Horvitz may get off point.

2.14 Motions. When a matter has been discussed fully, a person may make a motion with respect to the matter by stating, "Enough already. Let's get this over with. I say we vote."

2.15 Votes. Voting on motions may be by voice, by raising your right hand, by roll call or by secret ballot, depending on what the chair feels like. Proxy voting shall be permitted only for members of the firm's securities department.

2.16 Decisions. Matters coming before the committee shall be decided by majority vote. Ties go to the runner.

2.17 Effect of Decisions. Committee decisions shall be binding upon the firm, but need not be paid attention to.

The initial euphoria over the revised committee procedures was short-lived. A study conducted by the Productivity Committee six months after the rules were adopted revealed that committee meetings were lasting, on average, thirty-seven minutes longer since the effective date of the new rules. This was attributed by the study primarily to appeals to the Committee on Handbooks for interpretation of the rules. When a group of partners filed suit questioning the constitutionality of the provision that allowed only Sheldon Horvitz to speak off point, the partnership voted to rescind all of the rules. This rescission is currently being challenged by Sheldon Horvitz.

Tailor-made for Law

But what *did* get me interested in the law? Seems like a fair enough question to ask somebody reflecting on better than half a century of practice.

The answer is not what, but who: Cutter.

Lloyd Schneider was a neighbor. Cutter, he was called—a play on both his name, which meant "cutter," that is, "tailor," in German, and his prowess as a halfback in football. Cutter was my dad's age, probably a bit older, actually. But he was my friend. He lived in the big brick house on the corner of my block, together with his sister, Alice, who was an invalid. Cutter was a lawyer.

Each fall when I was growing up, Cutter would invite all of the kids on our block (actually, just the boys) over to the park on Saturday and Sunday afternoons for football practice. He always wore a three-piece suit and a pocket watch with a chain that he'd use to time the games. No matter how cold it was, he never wore an overcoat. Most days he'd wheel Alice over to watch, all bundled up in plaid woolen blankets, a World War I flier's hat—flaps down—and red boots with white fur on top. Alice loved those games. She always cheered for the team that was behind. Afterwards, we'd all tramp back to Cutter's house, where Alice would have baked us some chocolate chip cookies to go with the cocoa Cutter made.

Practice would begin with Cutter running us through a series of rigorous exercises and drills his college coach at Purdue had put the team through. After the drills, we'd choose up teams and play a game. Cutter refereed. Each time the ball changed hands, he'd gather us around him and review the plays that we'd just run. There might be fifteen or twenty plays, but Cutter could remember them all, in order, and point out exactly what we had done right or wrong in each. We all had the utmost respect for Cutter. It would never have occurred to any of us to question his word.

Cutter's tutelage influenced all of us, sometimes in ways it took us many years to appreciate. Most directly, six of us from the block went on to start on the Senn High School football team, including me. I played center. That got me used to looking at people upside down through my legs, a perspective that I think helped me throughout my legal career. One member of our team, Jim Stickle, even went on to star in college, as a halfback (much to Cutter's delight), though at Northwestern, not Purdue.

We all became students of the game. It wasn't until high school that I realized football rules did not require a break after each exchange of the ball to discuss the plays that had occurred on the previous series of downs. I'm sure it was Cutter's influence that made me huddle with young lawyers at my firm to replay each move we'd made on a deal (sometimes, I'm sure they thought, *ad nauseam*).

All of us on the football squad (we referred to ourselves as "Cutter's Crew," and Cutter had sweatshirts made for us with that name on them) knew that Cutter was a lawyer, though we had little idea what that meant. All we knew was the way he dressed: the three-piece suit and the gold watch and chain. Come to think of it, I suppose it's not impossible that the three-piece suit and gold watch and chain I wear today were influenced by Cutter. It is, after all, the watch he left me in his will. But Cutter never wore a bow tie—that's all mine.

In any case, when I turned fourteen I came to learn a bit more about what being a lawyer meant. My father was injured at his job, running a machine press in a leather foundry. For several months he was out of work and money was scarce around our home. Somehow, Cutter learned about that and offered me a job, working parttime at his law office, doing odds and ends. I, of course, jumped at the chance.

Looking back on that experience, I think I was most impressed with the way Cutter was treated by everyone— his clients, his secretary, the people to whom I delivered letters or packages. All held him in the highest esteem and would no more have questioned his word than would one of us in Cutter's Crew. Of the work he did, I, of course, had little idea, though he did permit me to read through documents, in my spare time. Those documents seemed to me very arcane (though that word would not have come to mind) and dull and complicated. My later experience proved this early assessment to be remarkably sound.

Through high school I continued to work with Cutter, and I maintained my contact with him during vacations after I left for college. Though, as I have said, I majored in philosophy, I did not seriously consider becoming a professor. The professorial life was rather too sedate and contemplative for me (although some of the stories I've since heard from my academic friends make me think that the world of the mind might well be a far more competitive environment than the one I chose).

When it came round to deciding what to do after college, I considered just heading out into the world, getting a job and trying to make my mark. But at the back of my mind, I knew that law school was also a possibility. I admired Cutter. And I liked the fact that he was admired by everyone he dealt with. As the first in my family to endure college, I felt that I'd earned some respect. I liked the esteem that I thought would be associated with becoming a lawyer.

I discussed my concern with Cutter, who listened

carefully and answered my questions, but expressed no opinion himself. I told him that I worried about the debt I would incur in going to law school. That debt would be piled atop the money I'd already borrowed to go to college. But in the end I applied, and not only was I accepted, I was offered a full scholarship. I didn't learn until much later that the scholarship they awarded me chanced to have been a gift to the law school from my former football coach.

Perhaps all of this surprises you a bit, my attachment to—perhaps even worship of—Cutter. You may have been misled by that cool, unemotional exterior of mine into thinking I was some one-dimensional, gruff old codger who waltzed alone through life right into the corner office of one of the country's most prestigious law firms. Not by a long shot. I've carved my success out of the rocks of experience, but I've had plenty of help along the way.

It's the mistake of every younger generation to think that only they are complex, that their predecessors led simple, uncomplicated lives. Well, I say hogwash to that. To be complicated, you don't need a computer and a fax machine, or even a photocopy machine. Remember, those things solve problems for you that we had to reckon with alone.

I *am* a feisty old critter, aren't I?

The Best of PALS

Prospective lawyers are not the only ones who lack role models, these days. Equally serious is the lack of role models that young lawyers find, once they arrive at the firm. Acutely aware of this problem, the FWS Committee on Associate Retention and Evaluation (CARE) sprang to action recently with this memo from CARE Chair Stephen Falderall.

To: All Partners
From: Stephen I. Falderall, CARE Chair
Re: Mentorship

Our young associates are floundering. If you doubt this, step outside your office and watch them flopping about in the hall. Not a pretty sight, especially at what we're paying them.

CARE has determined that the major reason for associate floundering is the lack of mentoring that our young associates receive today. Forty years ago, when our firm was ten lawyers, mentoring took place naturally. For the last thirty-five or so years, it hasn't taken place at all.

Recognizing this, CARE adopted the following resolution, 4-3: "RESOLVED that there's no time like the present to do something about the firm's mentoring problem." (Two of those voting 'nay' agreed that it was time that something be done about the problem, but could not in good conscience support the resolution because of their belief that there might yet prove to be another time like the present.) This memo sets forth our new Partner-Associate Liaison Strategy (PALS).

Introduction

Some partners may approach mentoring with a certain skepticism. "Why," they might ask, "is this necessary? *I* was able to make it in this firm without any sort of formal mentorship program," they might say, "so why can't associates today do the same thing, especially since we pay them so much money and they're supposed to be so damn smart? I'm very busy and I've got a lot of pressures on me—to bill, to develop clients, to write articles, to serve on firm committees, just to name a few," they might add. "Why do you have to dump another responsibility on me? Huh? And," they might continue, "it's not like I'm going to get any credit for this, either. I've got plenty of other things I'd rather do than mentor. Why don't you just leave me alone?" they might conclude.

CARE is happy you were able to get all of that off your chest. Venting is healthy. CARE understands your problems. After all, CARE is composed of partners, too. So now can we get on with mentoring?

Establishing the Mentor-Mentee Relationship

CARE wants to make our mentor system as natural as possible. As we know that many of our partners have not related to anyone—much less somebody a generation younger than them—in a decade or more, we list below several possible ways to greet your mentee:

RIGHT: "Hello, I'm _____. I'll be your mentor. Any questions?"

OKAY: "Like, hi. I'm like _____. I'll like be your mentor. Do you like have any questions for me?"

WRONG: "Under the recently established PALS program, I have been assigned by CARE to serve as your

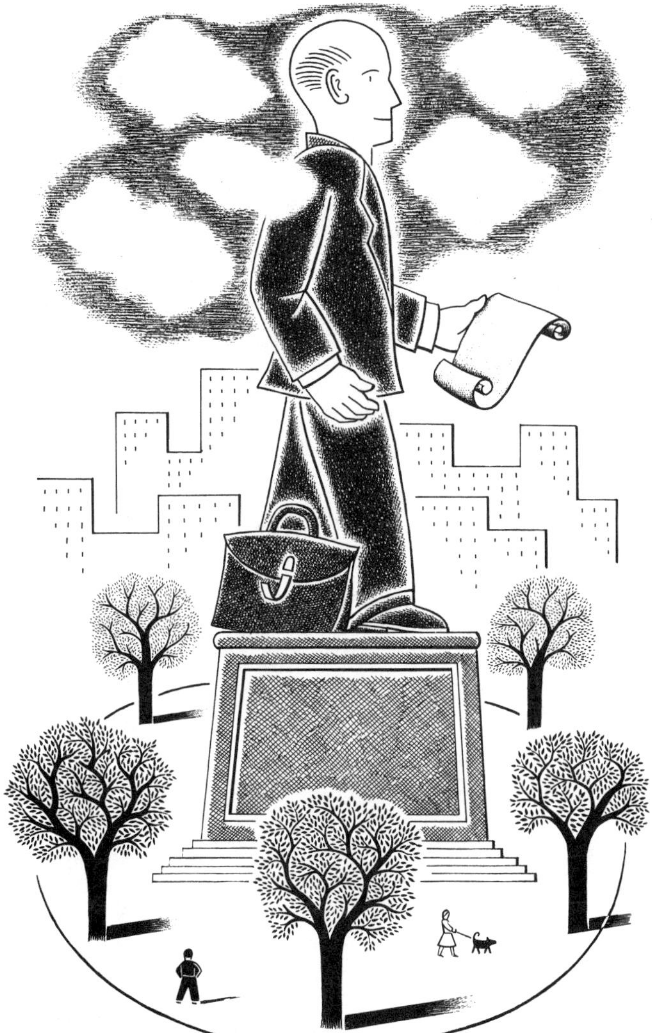

mentor, a fiduciary position that I am very happy to assume. I would like our relationship to be a very natural one, if that is acceptable to you. Should you have any interrogatories, you should feel free to pose them to me at a mutually convenient time."

Once you have greeted the mentee, you will want to try to break the ice. Set forth below are some icebreakers that you may find helpful:

- "Do you have much debt, coming out of law school?"
- "The Grateful Dead are quite a group, aren't they?"
- "I believe in a supernatural force that created the universe, do you?"
- "Which wines do you prefer— red, white or pink?"
- "I'm opposed to the indiscriminate use of nuclear weapons, are you?"
- "How about those Cubs?"
- "How about that Supreme Court?"

Of course, the above are merely suggestions. You should feel free to use them or not, as you see fit. You are trying to establish a bond with your mentee and there are many ways to accomplish that. Use whatever works for you (although CARE discourages bonding by walking down the hall quacking, and requesting your mentee to follow behind you).

CARE knows that it is easier to establish a relationship with somebody with whom you have something in common. Accordingly, we have assigned mentees by height, so that no mentee will be more than two inches taller or shorter than his mentor. Unfortunately, this meant leaving our new 6'7" associate, Rolf Zitz, unmentored. (But chances of anyone relating to Rolf were slim in any case.)

Duties of a Mentor

Because we want this relationship to be a natural one, we are not setting forth any absolute duties of a mentor. Nonetheless, these guidelines may be useful:

1. Take the mentee to lunch once every four weeks, on Thursday.

2. Schedule a half-hour meeting with the mentee every week (and don't have your secretary call to cancel it at the last minute because "something important came up").

3. Introduce the mentee to other presentable partners, if you can find any.

4. Even if you're unusually busy, stop by the mentee's office every other day, pop your head in and say "hi, hwarya," then move on before your mentee can answer.

5. Ask the mentee if he is happy with the work he is getting.

6. If the answer is "no," say, "That's a shame, I hope it improves."

7. Encourage your mentee by patting him on the top of the head and telling him you've been hearing good things about him (whether or not you have).

8. Flood your mentee with helpful advice, such as, "Rome wasn't built in a day" or "When the going gets tough, the tough get going" or "He who laughs last was pretty slow to get the joke."

Common Questions

We've tried to identify the common questions we believe mentors may have and to give you some common answers below:

Q: Does it matter if my mentee is of the opposite sex?

A: Certainly it matters.

Q: Should mentees be allowed to address mentors by their first names?
A: No, this is carrying friendliness a bit too far.

Q: When taking my mentee out to lunch, do I have to treat?
A: Not if the total bill exceeds $6. You may wish to offer to pay 55% of the bill, however, to show what a sport you are.

Q: Will I receive credit and recognition from the firm for the time I spend mentoring?
A: Yes, in a life to come.

Q: How long am I expected to serve as mentor?
A: 'Til the last to occur of the following: (a) mentee becomes partner, (b) mentee leaves the firm, (c) mentee reaches puberty, or (d) you die.

Q: If I do not like my mentee, can I get a new one?
A: Only if he or she is unused and you saved the receipt.

Q: What should I do if my mentee consumes too much of my time with stupid questions?
A: Propose him for partnership.

Conclusion

PALS will only work if you make it work. Chances are not good.

Shout It from the Highest Desktop

I damn near became a dentist. Not really, but it makes a pretty good chapter kickoff, doesn't it. Northwestern University School of Law is located right next to the dental school and, in my day, neither one of them had a sign. So we used to joke that it wasn't until midterm exams that part of our law school class realized they'd been attending the dental school. My class got together for our senior class gift and bought a fancy sign for the law school, to save future generations of lawyers from hearing about root canals.

Considering its ancient history, my first year in law school remains remarkably vivid for me. We had quite a collection of characters among my classmates—Wally who moonlighted at the funeral home, Fred who read dirty magazines inside his casebooks until our criminal law professor caught him one day, and Jack who sold copies of his course outlines for eight bucks a piece (a hefty price in that day). Wally became an ace litigator for a large firm, Fred went to the State Attorney's office, then became a judge, and Jack owns about half the downtown in his hometown in Iowa. But the characters I remember best were my professors, especially one of them.

To me, contracts has always been the alphabet of the law. And in Professor R. Higby Cedarhurst (who was known as "Higs" to his colleagues and, behind his back, to us), our morning section of contracts had a teacher who made sure that we minded our P's and Q's. From our large wooden desks, I remember gazing down at that tall, slender, septuagenarian (seventy seemed old to me, back then) as he paced back and forth in the pit created by the steep rows of Lincoln Hall. Peering through his round, wire-rimmed glasses, Cedarhurst would constantly shift his glance around the room, as if to assure himself that none of us was about to pounce on him from above.

With Higs as our guide, we began to explore just what made a contract. Both sides had to give something—"consideration." But what would suffice as consideration, Higs asked us—a peppercorn? Was a peppercorn of consideration enough, or did you need two peppercorns?

I love the word "peppercorn;" it's so colorful and alive. From the day Higs introduced me to it, that small, dried berry of the pepper entered my vocabulary and life forever. One of my law school classmates—Wally, the fellow who worked at the funeral home—gave me a jar of peppercorns as a gag graduation gift. I keep them on my desk. Don't know if law students today know about peppercorns, but all of my clients sure do.

Higs' influence on me extended beyond peppercorns, though. He taught me not to underestimate people, not to judge them by their appearance. Though physically old—Higs looked as if a stiff breeze would topple him—his repartee made it clear to all of us that it would take a hurricane to dislodge him mentally.

And he showed me the value of a wry sense of humor. I recall Higs stressing a point in one of our early classes. Speaking slowly and stroking his chin (as he always did), Higs told us, "Now this point is *so* important that I'm tempted to climb up on top of this desk and recite it to you . . . But I won't do that, because you wouldn't remember . . . Oh, you'd remember that I got up on the desk, all right, but you wouldn't remember the point." He was right, of course. I remember that he did *not* get up on the desk, but I don't remember the point.

Another time, I recall, Higs was making an announcement to our morning contracts section. He'd become a bit absent-minded—though I suspect that Higs was absent-minded at twenty, too. "I have an announcement to make," he started, then he paused and stroked his chin. "Now that I think about it, it's probably more relevant to the afternoon section . . . but since I started, I'll make it now anyway. . . .. Next Thursday, the afternoon section will not meet." Higs smiled at himself as our class broke into laughter at his perfectly irrelevant announcement.

But Higs brought much more than a sense of humor to his class. He brought a deep knowledge and love of his subject matter. Higs co-authored the casebook we used, and knew it backwards and forwards. Not only could he give you the case citation from the official reporter, he could cite the page number where it appeared in his casebook, all from memory. Probably twice a week the professor whose class followed Higs' had to usher Higs, and the group of students who had gathered around him, bodily out of the classroom. As he was being guided out, Higs would continue his discourse, seemingly oblivious to his changing venue.

Why am I telling you about Higs? These are not stories that reach out to you when you hear them, grab you by the shirt and say, "Listen here, this is something that's going to be important to you." Not at all. In fact, if I hadn't gotten off on a bit of a tangent here (no apologies for that), I might never have focused on them myself. But they are the type of little happenings that mold our lives.

As I've begun writing this book, I've thought more about what molds lives; more particularly, I suppose, what's molded mine. To what extent have I been the clay, to what extent the potter? To what extent have I been twirled around and around, propelled by a momentum I've never really tried to control or understand? These are not easy questions to answer.

Yes, answers are tough to come by. But often that's because the questions aren't even asked. We get so caught up in the moment that we never get beyond it. This problem may be even worse for younger lawyers. We old codgers might once have lived in an era in which we had time for reflection, but the pace today is so relentless that it's little wonder young lawyers are swept along by the current, with little time for anything but trying to avoid drowning.

I suppose that lack of a long-term view is a problem for any business. But it's compounded in law. How many other businesses do you know that see their principal assets ride down the elevator each night and divvy up everything they make at the end of each year? That sort of behavior is not exactly conducive to long-term thinking.

Anyway, I count myself fortunate to have this chance to step back and reflect a bit. Sometimes reflection causes you to think about some things you haven't thought about in a long time—like Higs. In his own way, I think Higs may have been one of the molders of my life. That might strike you as a bit odd. I don't seem much like the contracts professor type, and I'm not. But Higs represents more to me than his profession. Higs loved what he did. Passionately. And he wasn't afraid to show it. Even if showing it meant he risked looking like an ass.

I've always stood ready to climb up atop my desk to make a worthwhile point myself. I figure that if you've never looked like an ass, you probably haven't amounted to very damn much. So come, let us bray together.

In the Long Range . . .

At the Fairweather firm, we've recognized the impediments to law firms taking the longer view, which I've been pointing out. And we've tried to overcome them through our Long-Range Planning Committee, chaired ably by Herbert Gander. From the firm archives, I've reclaimed the minutes of the very first meeting of that committee, which are reproduced below.

Chairman Gander called the meeting of the Long-Range Planning Committee to order in the northeast conference room and welcomed all of the committee members. The committee members thanked Chairman Gander for welcoming them. Chairman Gander said that they were entirely welcome, that he regarded it his duty as Chairman to welcome everyone to meetings. Harriet Akers said that she thought the Chairman had been particularly gracious in his welcome and proposed a resolution commending the Chairman, which was adopted unanimously.

This being the committee's first meeting, reading of the minutes of the prior meeting and old business were both dispensed with, over Sheldon Horvitz's objection. The Chairman asked Sheldon why he objected. Sheldon said that, looking over the makeup of the committee, he felt that he would have to be a frequent dissenter and that he was just practicing.

The Chairman said that the first order of business was to choose a time and place for the next meeting. He suggested that the meeting be held in the same conference room one month hence. James Freeport objected, saying that he thought it would be more appropriate for a long-range planning committee to meet offsite, in a retreat setting, to contemplate the future. In our conference room, the present and past are too much with us, he opined. Helen Laser said that James had put that quite poetically and that she was inclined to support his suggestion, if a suitable offsite meeting place could be found.

"Well, I'm a member of the Moosetoe Lodge," said the Chairman, "and I'm sure we could arrange to have the meeting there."

"Excellent," said Hiram Miltoast. "I've never been there and would love to see the club."

"I object," said Sheldon.

"On what grounds?" the Chairman inquired.

"The Lodge discriminates."

"What makes you say it discriminates?" asked the Chairman.

"Odds. Most clubs discriminate against somebody."

"Well, it so happens that Moosetoe membership is open to everyone, Sheldon, so I guess that removes your objection."

"Absolutely not; every animal rights group in the country will be boycotting us if we meet at the Moosetoe. Meese are a protected species and their toes are very rare."

"There's no such thing as 'meese,' " said Hiram.

"Well I wouldn't be so sure. There are 'geese,' aren't there? And I'll bet there's even a big moosehead over the registration desk, shot by one of the members."

"Well, there is a moosehead, but it so happens that the moose in question died of a coronary, and there's a certificate on file to that effect at the Lodge."

"Big deal. My Uncle Melvin died of a coronary, but we

don't have his head up on some plaque. Aunt Sophie would never permit it."

The committee voted to have the next meeting at the Moosetoe, 5-1. The Chairman announced that the next order of business would be to adopt a mission statement for the committee.

"Why do we need a mission statement?" asked James.

"Because without a sense of our mission, how will we be able to plan?"

"I agree," said Sheldon. "I say we ought to focus on nuclear disarmament, the drug problem, the environment and crime in the streets. Unless we can make headway on those, I don't think there will be much of a long range to plan for."

"I think that we need to start with something a little less ambitious," suggested the Chairman.

"How about something like this," offered Hiram Miltoast: "The mission of the Long-Range Planning Committee of the law firm of Fairweather, Winters & Sommers shall be to formulate, adopt and implement, from time to time, sound and visionary plans that will maintain, support and strengthen the fabric of the law firm and contribute to the continued growth, prosperity and well-being of the firm and its lawyers through policies, actions and plans consistent with the basic raison d'être and historical values of the firm's founder, Stanley J. Fairweather."

"Hiram, you're a genius," said Harriet. "How did you ever come up with that off the top of your head?"

"Well, I have to admit that I didn't exactly make it up. I just finished serving on our church's long-range planning committee, and this is pretty much our mission, substituting 'Stanley Fairweather' for 'Jesus Christ.' "

"In any case, it sounds good to me, and I move its

adoption," said Harriet. And the mission statement was adopted, 5-1.

"So now I guess we start planning," said Helen.

"Not quite," said the Chairman. "First we have to break into subcommittees."

"Break into subcommittees?" complained James. "But we only have six members to begin with."

"Doesn't matter," said the Chairman. "Long-range planning is far too large and complicated a topic for the whole committee to tackle in the first instance."

"Okay then, but what will the subcommittees be?"

"I was thinking of business, lawyer development, central office planning, branch offices of the future, and human resources."

"But that's only five subcommittees, and there are six of us," Harriet pointed out.

"Since I'm chair of the committee, the five of you can each be chair of one of the subcommittees."

"And you can be an ex-officio member of each," said Sheldon, enthusiastically.

"But for each of our subcommittees, the firm already has a committee. Won't we be stepping on their toes?" asked Harriet.

"Not if we're careful," said the Chairman. "You see, they only look at short- or medium-range issues. We look at the long range."

"Well, how do we know where medium range ends and long range begins? Is it five years, ten?" asked James.

"No, I don't think we can do it that mechanically," said the Chairman. "Medium range may be one thing for one area and another for a different area."

"Then this gets very confusing," said Hiram. "There must be some way of defining our jurisdiction."

"I've got it," said Sheldon.

"You do? Okay, let's hear it," said the Chairman.

"The other firm committees have jurisdiction of anything capable of being implemented now or in the foreseeable future. We have jurisdiction of whatever is so vague, speculative or unlikely as to not be worth the time of the other committees."

Though the other members of the committee found something distressing in Sheldon's formulation, they had to admit that it captured their authority precisely. The formulation was adopted, 6-0.

"Well, we'd better get started planning soon, before some of the things we talk about become relevant," said the Chairman. "I think we've accomplished enough for our first meeting."

The motion to adjourn carried, 5-1.

Bachelorhood Blues

Seems impossible that I graduated from law school more than fifty-five years ago, but that's what the diploma up on my wall says—LL.B, 1937. And diplomas don't lie.

Of course, today I'd be a doctor. I don't mean a medical doctor, since I don't have the stomach for that. No, I'd be a juris doctor if I graduated today. In fact, I could be a doctor (juris) right now, if I wanted to. My law school gave me the chance to send in my diploma for a new one. But I turned them down flat. Bachelor's plenty good enough for me. Besides, they wanted to charge me twenty bucks for a new diploma. The nerve!

I'm a bachelor in more than my law degree, though. I have been for over fifty years now. I guess you could say that I tried divorce before it became fashionable. I shouldn't make light of that, I know. Divorce isn't funny. But it has been over fifty years; you get used to something in that amount of time. And if there's one thing I've learned in life, it's not to cry too long over spilt milk, even if you're the one who spilled it. Besides, even without the divorce I wouldn't be married to Harriet now. She's been dead thirty years.

So where did I go wrong?

Y'know, I'd as soon stay away from this topic altogether. And I thought about doing that. I told myself that this is supposed to be a book about my legal career, not my personal life. But it's not so easy to separate the two.

So I've decided to tell you about Harriet, at least briefly. Even if it's none of your damn business.

We were married just before I started law school, Harriet and me. We'd met—at a square dance, I still remember it—my junior year in college, through a mutual friend. From the first night we met, neither one of us dated anyone else. Love, I suppose.

Ours was, I guess, a fairly typical relationship back then. Harriet pursued one of the few professions open to women then, teaching. We were attracted to one another physically, and we enjoyed some of the same things— baseball, cooking, walking in the woods. Ours was not a particularly mature relationship. But whose is, at that age? Strikes me as odd that they have a minimum age for driving, but not marrying. I'd set it around sixty, I think; maybe fifty, with parental consent. That would take care of our overpopulation problems, too.

Anyway, Harriet supported us while I was in law school. I worked parttime with Cutter to earn some extra money. And we got by pretty well.

After I graduated, we decided to have a child. Harriet decided, really. I did not oppose it, though I had no idea in the world what having a child meant.

We had the child, Juliete. Juliete was Harriet's child. I had the law, which consumed almost all of my waking hours; Harriet had Juliete. We had a deal: Harriet didn't write my briefs, and I didn't change Juliete's. Oh, on a sunny weekend afternoon we would walk Juliete through the park in her pram, together. And I smiled and shared willingly in the compliments that admiring passersby offered. (She did look a lot like me, but fortunately outgrew it in time.) But I did not participate. I had the law; Harriet had Juliete. As we did at our first square dance, Harriet and I do-si-doed through these first years together, our backs to one another.

For a few years this arrangement worked well enough, or at least it seemed to me that it did. But gradually, Harriet decided she wanted a husband. I could not—or did not care to—understand what the hell she meant by that. I see now, of course. I could hold my liquor (I've never been a big drinker, anyway), but I could not hold my work. Unfortunately, there was no WA (Workaholics Anonymous) chapter around. I probably wouldn't have joined if there were, though; I had too much work to do.

Anyway, divorce is no picnic (or, at least, a damn expensive one). But then, neither is marriage. In fact, come to think of it, neither is a picnic such a picnic. You've got to prepare all that food, lug it to the car, worry about the hot stuff staying hot and the cold stuff cold, spilling things on the blanket, the bugs, the weather . . . So maybe nothing's a picnic . . . or everything is.

Truth is, looking back, nothing really went wrong with Harriet and me. I just plain wasn't ready for marriage. I wasn't mature enough. In fact, I still may not be. But at least I've had the good sense to realize that and not do it over and over again, like some folks do. And Harriet survived pretty well without me.

After our divorce, she moved with Juliete to Los Angeles, where her parents lived. A few years later, Harriet remarried. I had only sporadic contact with Juliete over the years; somewhat more, recently, because of Maggie, my granddaughter.

Maggie is a lawyer. In a way, I may have been Maggie's Cutter. I will tell you more about her, later. Maggie—bless her—has had the curiosity (or, perhaps, perversity) to seek out her grandfather. Through her I think I've finally discovered what having a child means.

We all have holes in our lives. Mine is a fairly large one, as you see. At first I tried to plug that hole through total immersion in my work. But that, of course, was foolish. We have personal needs and we have professional needs. One cannot substitute for—though each must accommodate—the other.

In the end, it comes down to a pretty simple notion—that lawyers are people. They look like people, they behave like people and they respond like people. The law firm that recognizes that reality comes out ahead in the long run.

There is danger on the other side of the ledger as well, though. I have seen plenty of firms that have tried to become families to their lawyers. And it doesn't work. Law firms aren't families, they're businesses. If they try to provide what only a family can offer, they are bound to fail.

Now, even though it didn't work for me, I'm not one who believes that marriage and the practice of law are incompatible. Not completely, anyway. You've got to want them both pretty badly to make a go of it, though. In quite a number of the marriages that I've seen work, lately, both spouses are lawyers. To each his own, I suppose, but give me bachelorhood over that, any day.

Oddly enough, a lot of lawyers in my firm seem to come to me for counseling on this marriage thing. It's as if they're saying, "You botched the hell out of it, Stanley; now tell us how to avoid doing what you did." Of course, none of them has had the bad sense to put it that way. (At least none who is still with the firm.)

One thing I tell them is to cultivate dispensability. I find that most lawyers do the opposite. They have the need to think themselves indispensable to their clients. Then, when any conflict arises between personal and professional obligations, the latter inevitably wins out, as they think that only they can handle their clients' needs. I tell my lawyers that the only one who's indispensable around here is me.

So, I'm a bachelor of laws, and a bachelor of life—and likely to remain both, I guess. You never know, though;

I'm a handsome-enough devil, Maggie tells me. Maybe when I turn ninety I'll settle down again, with some young bimbo—of eighty-seven.

Anything Goes

One way the Fairweather firm considered trying to cultivate dispensability in its lawyers was through adopting a sabbatical policy. The policy evolved from a meeting of CHIP, the Committee on Health in Practice. Minutes of the meeting are set forth below:

Chairman Vance "Rip" Winkle called the meeting to order at noon, inviting the members to partake of the buffet lunch of tofu, yogurt, salad, bananas and prune juice.

Committee member Gerald Forspiel asked whether it might be possible to have something a little more substantial for their next lunch.

"Such as what?" asked Ruth Tender.

"Such as cheeseburgers, french fries, pickles, Coke and brownies," replied Forspiel.

"Sounds good to me," Alexander Pouts agreed. "I don't see why we have to eat this miserable crap every meeting."

"This 'miserable crap,' as you put it, happens to be extremely healthy," said Sylvia Wurrier, "and our committee should be setting an example for the rest of the firm."

"Well I feel hypocritical," said Gerald. "I'm so hungry after each of our meetings that as soon as the meeting is over, I rush down to the drugstore and buy three Snickers bars and wolf them down."

"Could you pick up a couple for me?" asked Alex. "I've got another meeting right after we adjourn."

"Sure, no problem."

"I think Sylvia's right about our setting an example," said the Chair. "People walk by the conference room and see all of this healthy food on the buffet. It makes a good impression."

"Well, we can still have all of this healthy food on the buffet," said Gerald. "I don't object to that. I object to having to *eat* it. Hell, I'm even willing to hold my cheeseburger on my lap, under the table, so that nobody passing by the conference room can see it."

"We have almost this exact discussion every meeting," complained Sylvia. "Seems to me it's a big waste of time, especially when we have important things, like a sabbatical policy, on the agenda."

"You're right," said Rip. "I'd like to move on to that now. It's your proposal, Sylvia, so why don't you introduce it?"

"Happy to. I think it's time we adopted a sabbatical program. It would have many benefits to the firm."

"Name one," challenged Alex.

"Well, for one thing it would give people a chance to renew themselves."

"I didn't even realize we had to renew; I thought we were checked out for life."

"You know what I mean. Law is a very draining profession. It's good to be able to step away from it every once in a while. People would come back refreshed, ready to work, and be even more productive."

"They might get so refreshed that they wouldn't come back at all. We could refresh ourselves right out of a law firm," said Alex.

"No, fortunately our firm has not been doing well enough financially to allow our partners to contemplate that," said Rip.

"Refreshing is nice, but not exactly a compelling

reason. Vacations refresh, too. What else would your sabbatical accomplish, Sylvia?" asked Alex.

"I think it would make for a better relationship between our partners, more trust."

"How would it do that?"

"Well, if partners were going to leave on sabbatical, they would have to share their clients, introduce them to other partners who could service them while the partner was away. Otherwise, when the partner returned, the client would be gone."

"That sounds appealing. But your idea would be very expensive, wouldn't it?" asked Alex.

"There would be some costs involved," Sylvia admitted, "but I think that it would be more than offset by the benefits. Aside from those I've already mentioned, a sabbatical policy would be helpful in attracting talented lawyers to our firm and then in getting them to remain. We also could vicariously enjoy the experience of others' sabbaticals."

"Well, if we adopted something like what you suggest, who would be eligible for a sabbatical?" asked Rip.

"Lawyers who had been partners for a specified length of time, say eight years."

"Looking over the list of our lawyers, it appears that about two-thirds of our partners could go on sabbatical—including virtually the entire tax and litigation departments. I can see our clients calling with a tax question and being told, I'm terribly sorry, but our tax department is on sabbatical, would you mind calling back in a few months. That might make it a little tough for us to turn a profit," said Alex.

"We'd have to figure out some way of staggering sabbaticals to make sure that not too many people went at once and that each area of practice was covered," said Sylvia.

"How would we go about doing that?" asked Gerald.

"I suppose we could develop some sort of application form that people who wanted to go on sabbatical would fill out and submit to a sabbatical committee for decision."

"Along with three letters of recommendation?" asked Gerald.

"And we could hire an educational testing company to develop a standardized Sabbatical Aptitude Test that we could administer, and Stanley Kaplan could develop a preparatory course," added Alex.

"Go ahead and make fun," said Sylvia.

"Would everyone have to take a sabbatical?" asked Ruth.

"Absolutely," said Sylvia. "It's for their own good, and for the good of the firm."

"Well, some people might not see it that way and 'forget' to take their sabbatical," Gerald suggested.

"No problem, we just get Stanley to remind them, gently. He could walk into the person's office and announce, 'Forspiel, you're on sabbatical. You've got two hours to get out of here—see you in a few months.'"

"And what if Stanley doesn't go along with that, and decides that our most successful lawyers should have the right to balk at compulsory time off?"

"Well, I suppose it wouldn't be so terrible if some of our most productive lawyers didn't take their sabbaticals," said Sylvia.

"So, in other words," said Alex, "this program is really a benefit to reward our mediocre and lousy lawyers, since they'll have no trouble getting away and, presumably, no compunction about taking the time off."

"Don't be ridiculous, Alex. Presumably, nobody who's been a partner at our firm for eight years would be a lousy or mediocre lawyer."

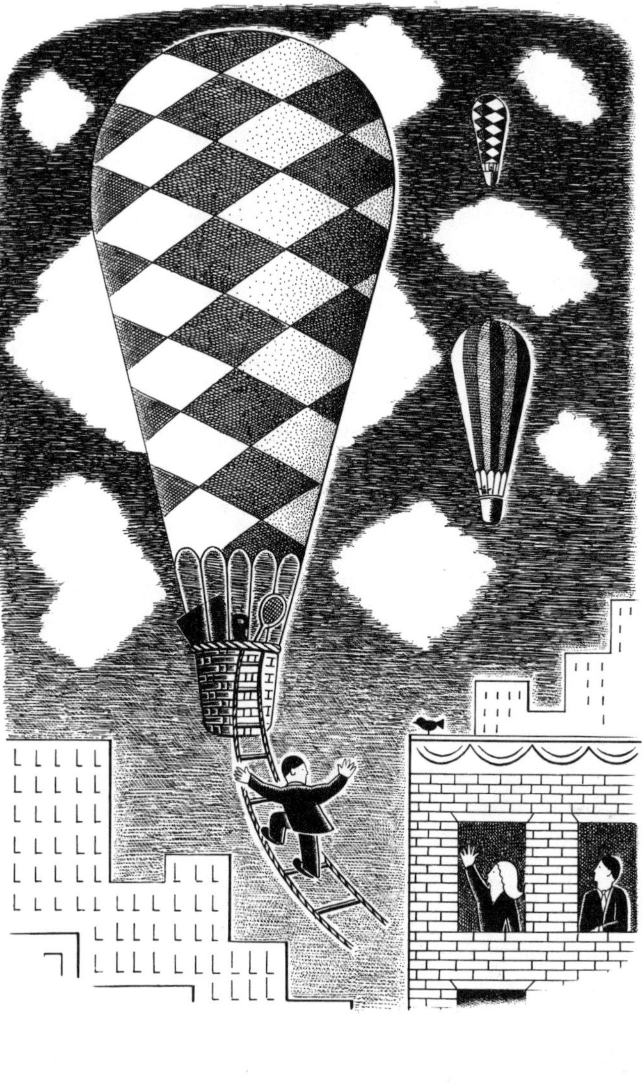

"Right, Sylvia, and please say hello to the Tooth Fairy for me next time you run into her."

"Sylvia, what could lawyers choose to do with their sabbatical time?" asked Ruth. "Would it have to be law related?"

"No, they could do whatever they wanted. If they wanted to go off and teach law, or write a legal treatise, that would be fine. But if they just wanted to travel, that would be okay, too."

"Anything they want, eh?" said Gerald, sounding somewhat interested, for the first time.

"Yup, anything," said Sylvia.

"So, if I wanted to, say, go to Australia and dive the Great Barrier Reef for a few months, that would be okay?" said Alex.

"Sure would, doesn't sound so bad, does it, Alex?"

"No, it doesn't."

"You said that others could enjoy these sabbaticals vicariously, Sylvia. How would they be able to do that?" asked Ruth.

"That would be easy, in my case," said Alex. "I'd take reels of slides, and everybody could come to the conference room and enjoy them while I described them. We could even sell popcorn, which would make the Finance Committee happy."

"Forget it," said Gerald. "I was starting to get interested in this idea, but not anymore. I may have to eat the lousy health food you serve at these meetings, but I'll be damned if I'm voting for an expensive new program that's going to require me to watch Alex's slides. It may leave *him* refreshed, but the rest of us'll be bored silly. You've got to draw the line somewhere."

Seasoning Lawyers to Taste

At first I ate out a lot, after Harriet left. Talk about a rut to get into, that's it. Not to mention all the weight you gain. I figured I had two choices: eat frozen low-cal meals four days a week, or learn to cook.

The idea of learning to cook intrigued me, probably because it seemed such an improbable thing for a guy like me to be doing. Now my granddaughter, Maggie, would tell me how sexist that remark is, and it is. (I'll have to get in a few words about women lawyers later, even though that's bound to get me into trouble.) But it also happens to be true. Even today, not that many men cook. Back in the early 1940s, almost none did. Except chefs.

So I went into a bookstore and picked out a cookbook. I remember looking around the store to make sure that nobody I knew was watching me. It felt almost pornographic. (Now, *there's* an idea for a surefire bestseller: *Lunching Naked*, by Chef Z.)

When I got the book home and started to read, I discovered that cookbooks (or at least this one) are written for people who know how to cook. How do you sauté or baste? what's au gratin? how do you fold in sauce? what is a corer the size of a small biscuit cutter? Over a week or so, I stumbled through several recipes, with results that would not give a master chef reason to pause for fear that I might trot off with his job. I began to suspect that cookbooks were written by the same sadists who write directions for assembling model airplanes, and that my cooking career might end as abruptly as my models had—against a wall.

To avoid that fate, I determined to seek out a cooking class, preferably one outside of my neighborhood. After a couple of weeks of keeping my eyes open, I spotted one that seemed appropriate, called, as I recall, "Cooking for the Novice."

My classmates were seven newlywed women, all of whom were less novice than I. I felt a bit out of place, to say the least, and even thought about quitting. But my classmates took me under their wing, made me more or less the class pet. (I was the only member of the class to have two dishes named after me—the Fairweather Fricassee of Fowl and Stanley's 'Sparagus Speciale.)

So I stuck it out, and wound up learning more about the practice of law in that novice cooking class than I did in three years of law school. They don't teach you about the practice of law in law school, or at least they didn't in my day. From what I see of the students coming out of law school, it's not much better today, even with all of those clinical programs.

"But how can you learn about practicing law from cooking?" you may ask. And that question itself speaks volumes about why so many lawyers have problems in the practice. They think that the only way you can learn about practicing law is in law school and in law books and from other lawyers. Truth is, you can learn about practicing law from most anything in life, because law encompasses all of life. At its best it does, anyway. And that's the reason I've stuck with it all of these years.

But there I go again, waxing philosophical, law encompassing life and all. So let me get back to specifics, to cooking, and what I learned from that. First off, I learned that nothing's as simple as it seems. I didn't think that cooking would be a big deal, when I bought that cookbook.

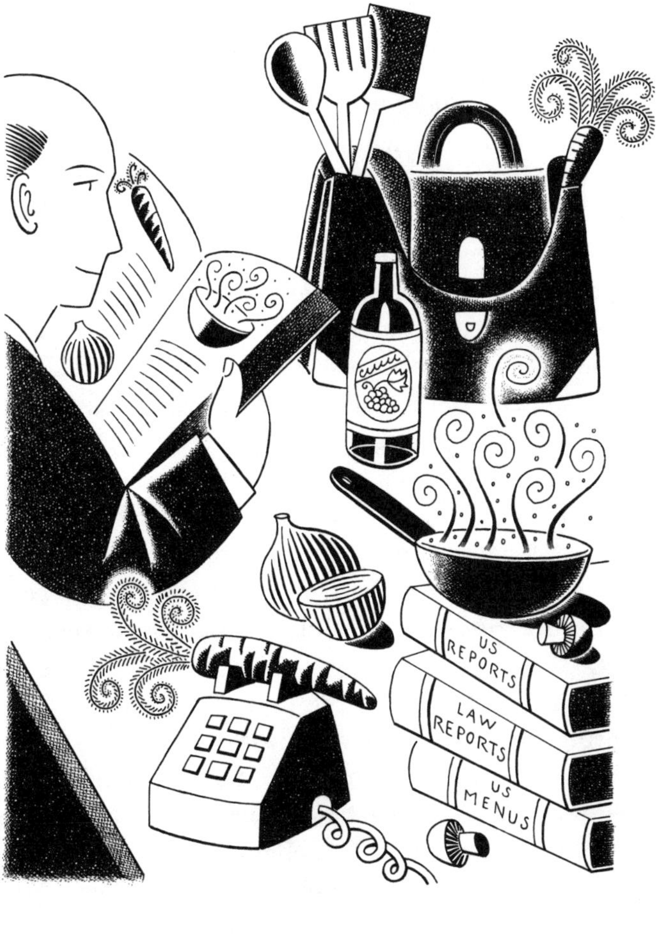
US REPORTS
LAW REPORTS
US MENUS

Turned out there was a whole lot more to it than I'd thought. Taught me a healthy respect for the people who knew how to do it.

I also learned about mentoring by being a mentee—and a totally ignorant one at that. The women in the class helped me out, and somehow did it without making me feel like a complete dolt. I have tried to apply some of those same techniques in the mentoring I've done at the firm.

I also learned that cooking takes a lot of time. You can't rush it. You may get something done cooking it at 400 degrees for an hour instead of 325 for an hour and a half, but it sure won't taste the same. You've got to show some patience, let those juices build over time.

And not everything works right the first time around. Even with a recipe, you need some trial and error to work out the kinks. You need to modify things based on your experience and on what you have to work with. Same is true in law. The best form in the world is not going to produce the result you want without some serious tinkering.

I used to think that the only thing that mattered in preparing a meal was how it tastes. The more I learned about cooking, though, the more I realized that the way something looks is almost as important as how it tastes. And the way things look to a client is important, too. Your letter or contract may say all of the right things, but if it looks as if it's been scratched out by some hen, or if you look as if you dressed in the dark, or if your office looks as if it's about to be condemned by the health authorities, don't count on seeing that client around for very long.

I could go on about what I learned from cooking—how the quality of the final product depends upon the quality of the ingredients that you put in to start, how the different courses of the meal must complement and build upon each other, how you can never please everyone's taste with any dish that's (so to speak) worth its salt, how a dash of spice can make all the difference, how cooking is an international language and so on and so forth. And all of this, of course, bears on the practice of law.

Perhaps I've made my point.

I don't want to suggest that all of this occurred to me in my first novice cooking class—or in my third, for that matter. (At the time, I was too busy bolixing up some perfectly fine recipes.) Nor do I want to suggest that I recognized all of this and incorporated it consciously into my law practice (though I wish I had). But we are, all of us, the sum of our experiences. And they affect us in ways that we cannot begin to know or understand. So I feel perfectly confident that I am correct when I say that I became a better (and more patient) lawyer as I became a better cook.

And now I have to break for lunch. I'm going to zap some soup in the firm microwave. You have to know when to fuss over something and when to zap the sucker, eat, and get on with it. There, that's another cooking lesson for you.

Res Ipsa Lunchitor

Like most everything else, eating has changed over the years at Fairweather, Winters & Sommers. Used to be, all of the lawyers could go out together to grab a bite at Winkles, the local eatery in the basement of our building. But Winkles is gone. And they never had a table that would seat 154, anyway.

These days, figuring out how to feed people at the firm presents a big logistical problem. Each day we have meetings that require food-and-beverage service. And then there's the problem of what to do with those who aren't in meetings. So we established a committee to consider the problem. Below is a transcript of the meeting of COKE, the ad hoc Committee on Cafeteria or Kitchen Evaluation.

"I'd like to begin the meeting by resigning as chair," announced COKE chair, Susan Pritchet.

"But why, we haven't done anything yet?" asked Harvey Holdem.

"Because I think it's very sexist appointing a woman as chair of a committee that has to do with food service. You never see women chairs of other committees."

"Oh yes you do," corrected Lionel Hartz. "When we moved offices, Fawn was chair of the ad hoc Decorating Committee, weren't you, Fawn?"

"I was, and that just proves Susan's point."

"That's right," said Rachel Steinberg. "And look at the composition of this committee: a majority are women. What other committee can say that?"

"Judging from the way this meeting is going so far," said Harvey, "it's a good thing the answer is 'none.' Look, Susan, if you don't want to be chair, I certainly would be honored to take the position."

"Fine," said Susan.

"Now, Susan, would you please be secretary and . . ."

"Absolutely not."

"Okay, okay. Jeez. Lionel, would you please act as secretary."

"It would be my honor and pleasure, Mister Chairman."

"Good, now can we please get on with the issue—whether to install a kitchen or a cafeteria."

"I'd like a cafeteria," said Lionel. "That way we wouldn't have to bring food from home."

"But a cafeteria would be very expensive," said Rachel. "We'd have to devote a tremendous amount of space to it, hire a whole host of new employees and basically get into the restaurant business. And if people didn't use it, we could lose a bundle."

"We'd have to sell people on the cafeteria, convince them to use it," said Harvey.

"How would we do that?" asked Fawn.

"I'm not sure, we'd have to use our imaginations."

"Oh-oh, that's trouble," said Lionel.

"We could run promotions, get endorsements," continued Harvey.

"Promotions?" asked Fawn.

"Sure. Maybe you give people a letter of the alphabet each time they eat at the cafeteria, and when they can spell out Fairweather, Winters & Sommers they win a free coke."

"Great idea. It would take at least twenty-five visits to win a coke—that should be a real grabber, Harv."

"I'm just thinking aloud, Fawn. Maybe we run a

lottery, and whoever picks numbers that match the firm's income for the month wins a free meal."

"We couldn't do that, Harv," said Rachel. "The firm's income is secret."

"If we're going to draw people into the cafeteria, we need to come up with a name for it," said Susan. "Any ideas, Lionel?"

"I thought we'd call it the Fairweather, Winters & Sommers Cafeteria."

"Catchy," said Susan. "Do you think we can do any better than that?"

"How about something French-sounding, like Le Café du Fairweather, Winters & Sommers?" offered Harvey.

"Chic, Harv," said Susan. "Any other ideas?"

"Maybe we should go with a legal-sounding name, like Res Ipsa Lunchitor," Rachel suggested.

"Not bad, Rache. Good slogan possibilities—'Feed Your Face at Res.' "

"I've got a better idea, how about 'Chez Stanley.' " Harvey suggested.

"Perfect," said Susan.

"What would we have on the menu?" asked Fawn.

"Cheeseburgers would be nice, with grilled onions," said Harvey.

"Maybe we could name dishes after lawyers at the firm," said Lionel. "Steak tartar could be a Nails Burger."

"Or after committees," suggested Harvey. "Bread and water could be the Finance Committee Fantasy, and tofu and yogurt could be CHIP's Choice."

"Have we decided whether this cafeteria would be for lawyers only, or whether everyone at the firm would be entitled to eat there?" asked Rachel.

"Are you kidding, it would have to be only for lawyers. You don't think we're going to eat with secretaries and people from the mailroom, do you?" asked Harvey.

"Why, how openminded of you, Harvey," said Susan. "It's that kind of attitude that has contributed to such fantastic *esprit de corps* among our support staff."

"Well, I didn't mean that there would be anything *wrong* with eating with the support staff. But that sort of . . . fraternizing . . . you know . . . it's not healthy in the long run. It breeds too much, well, familiarity . . . you know."

"Yes, I know very well, Harvey. I don't think you'd have to worry much about fraternizing, though. I can't imagine that the support staff would be rushing for a spot at your table."

"I suppose it would be okay, if we had separate sections."

"How would we price food at the cafeteria?" asked Fawn.

"We'd have to be below market, so the firm would have to subsidize the cost of meals," said Susan.

"Subsidize? The Executive Committee would never go for that. I was thinking that we could turn a profit on it," said Lionel.

"Well, we might be able to turn a profit on it, even if we subsidize the meals," said Susan.

"That makes no sense at all," said Lionel. "How could that be?"

"By having a cafeteria in the office, people would spend less time away for lunch. That should mean more billable time for lawyers and more productivity for the staff. The firm could more than make up the cost of the subsidy that way."

"And despite Harvey's attitude, the cafeteria might help build some camaraderie in the office," added Fawn.

"Well, if we can make money on it, build camaraderie and give people the convenience of eating in the building for less than they could at a restaurant, why not do it?" asked Lionel.

"Sounds right to me," said Susan. "I move that we recommend that the firm establish a cafeteria."

"I second the motion," said Lionel.

"There is one small problem, however," said Harvey.

"What's that?" asked Susan.

"Our lease."

"What do you mean, our lease?"

"The lease prohibits having a food service facility on premises."

"Harvey, you mean you knew that all along?"

"Of course. I read the lease before the meeting. After all, I *am* a lawyer."

"But if you knew the lease prohibited a cafeteria, why did you let us talk about it for the entire meeting without saying anything."

"Well, I used to be a member of the Long-Range Planning Committee. And in that committee we spent all of our time talking about things that had no practical application at all. So this seemed natural. Besides, if we ever move to a building that permits cafeterias, we're set; we've covered all the pros and cons already."

Risk Not, Want Not

Here is my sermon on money: Money is not the root of all evil. But, on the other hand, neither does it lead to grace. In law firms, money causes its share of problems. But then, so does a lack of money.

Well, at least it's a short sermon.

I've always thought that we lawyers weren't born to be rich. And that's fair enough, if you ask me. Or at least it used to be fair enough. There's some justice, I think, in the old-fashioned notion that those who take the risk should reap the greatest reward. And lawyers are not risktakers. If they were, they'd be investment bankers.

The reason we're not risktakers is that to be a risktaker you've got to be able to make a decision. And we lawyers are not very good at that. Just read some of the proceedings of my firm's committees and see how hung up we get on process, on considering all of the possible issues (no matter how irrelevant they may prove to be), on postponing the inevitable. Of course, we come by that honestly, through our legal education, which rewards spotting—not resolving—issues. Real life, on the other hand, I've found, tends to reward resolving issues.

Speaking of investment bankers (as I believe I was a short while ago), there was a time in the 80s when there was perceived by some to be a competition for talent between law firms and investment banks. We large law firms kept upping our salaries each year, in part, we said, because of the competition from investment banks. That notion always struck me as mildly hilarious. For starters, the temperament required of lawyers and investment bankers is about as similar as that required of chess players and auto racers. For another, any student who was attracted to a law firm rather than an investment bank by the increase in law firm starting salaries didn't have a very bright future in investment banking in any case, since he didn't know which was higher, a five-figure or a six-figure salary.

Once upon a time, one of our corporate partners—T. William Williams "T-Bills"—was lured away for a short stretch by the siren sounds of one of our small former investment banking clients. Old T-Bills thought he was going to make it big, real fast. Unfortunately for Bill, the stock market turned south, big-time, shortly after he joined the investment bank. After months of sleepless nights, T-Bills got up the gumption to come see me and ask if we'd have him back. I told him we'd be glad to, on one condition—that he get rid of the forty pairs of suspenders he'd bought in order to look like an investment banker. Last year I threw T-Bills a surprise sixtieth birthday party and asked everyone to bring a gift—the gaudiest pair of suspenders they could find.

So anyway, as I was saying, investment bankers got rich. And businessmen got rich. And lawyers did quite okay. And that was as it should be (or seemed it should be). And nobody complained very much. After all, we lawyers belong to a profession—and that's worth something, isn't it?

Now, during all of this time lawyers at some law firms were making more money than their classmates at other firms. But even that didn't seem to bother anybody very much, especially since nobody knew for sure who was doing real well and who was doing only moderately well. You might ride home on the train next to a fellow lawyer and suspect that he was outearning you. After all, there was that Mercedes he drove to the train every day, the vacations he took to the islands each January and the two-story addition he'd put on his house last summer. But who knew for sure; maybe his spouse just inherited a pile of money.

But then we ate of the tree of knowledge (or at least what we devoured was printed on former trees). A spate (I'd say a plague) of legal publications descended upon us. And all of a sudden, our worst suspicions were confirmed. That fellow on the train had not married an heiress. That 300SL, that mid-winter tan, that vaulted-ceiling family room—they were all paid for out of the earnings of his law practice. "Why him, and not me?" fourteen pairs of eyes seemed to ask in unison as they peered up from the legal periodical they were perusing on the train. And fourteen mouths asked the same question aloud at partnership meetings around the city, including ours.

I remember partnership meetings when those first legal rags started appearing. One of my partners (out of an excess of human kindness, I'm not going to mention his name) raises his hand and says, "Did you see where the guys down on the thirty-second floor are making an average of about thirty grand a year more than we are?"

"Percifal," I said, "you feeding the wife and kids?"

"Yup," he said.

"Making the mortgage payments?"

"Uh-huh."

"Took a pretty nice vacation abroad last year, as I recall?"

"Yes, we did, Stan."

"And didn't you and the missus buy yourselves a condo down in Palm Beach?"

"Yes."

"Then I'd just as soon not hear about what the guys on thirty-two are pulling down, if you don't mind."

"No, not at all. I just thought it was an interesting tidbit I'd share with my partners is all."

"Well, we sure appreciate your thinking of us like that, Percifal."

I can't recall that we ever had much discussion of those publications' reports in subsequent partnership meetings.

Other firms, though, were not so fortunate. Percifal's tidbits loosed a firestorm of activity in the legal community. Rainmakers took their rain to other locales (generally where the average annual rainfall was already tropical). Executive committees opened new offices around the country and the world. Finance committees tightened the spending reins. Hiring committees trolled for bodies at levels they had never before explored. (And when work trailed off, associates and partners were sent packing.) Compensation systems were altered to reward those who controlled the business. Outside seers were consulted to show firms the route to an improved bottom line.

And all of this loosened the fabric of law firms. It seemed to at least blur, if not erase, the line between the legal profession and business. And once this line was blurred (or erased), there seemed less reason for lawyers to be content with their economic lot. So greed set in.

This is not a pretty tale I am telling, I know. And it makes me sad to tell it. No one change made a big difference. But one thing built upon another, often unaware of its impact. Let me give you an example of what I mean.

To maximize profits, we tried to increase our hourly rates as much as possible. At some point, of course, clients resisted these increases. We then sought to pass along costs, in lieu of raising hourly rates. Traditionally, firms had charged clients for out-of-pocket expenses, such as long-distance phone calls or travel incurred on the client's behalf. Soon, though, we began charging for photocopying, secretarial overtime, word processing, firm messengers and the like. It's not that these were not legitimate expenses, costs of servicing the client's needs. But then, so too were pens, pencils, stationery, paper clips, etc. (Maybe I shouldn't say that, even in jest. Next thing I know, our Finance Committee will push for a paper-clip surcharge.)

In my view, charging our clients for all of these expenses subtly changed the nature of the attorney-client relationship, cheapening our overall professional services. A similar change occurred in the airline industry, I think, when airlines began charging passengers for drinks. That converted flight attendants into cashiers and, in the process, altered (cheapened) the experience of flying.

To me, the saddest part is not that we law firms have focused on money. Money has always been important to us lawyers, I think. What's sad is that so many of us have allowed money to displace all of the other values in the practice of law.

But I've got a funny feeling that all of that may change in the 90s. Hell, with the economic squeeze, values may be all we law firms have left.

Pencils Aren't Peanuts

As clients began to balk at continuing to absorb the increased expenses of the firm in the form of increased hourly rates and surcharges, our firm began to look for ways to control its expenses. In fact, at one meeting of the Fairweather, Winters & Sommers Finance Committee devoted to expenses, emotions raged so strongly that the meeting disintegrated into a name-calling contest. Rather than permit that to continue, Finance Committee chair F. Fred Feedrop took the time-honored step of suggesting that a subcommittee be formed to deal with expense control. This led to some immediate questions.

"Who's going to serve on the subcommittee?" asked committee member Gary Swath.

"And more important, what's it going to be called?" asked Lionel Hartz.

"I'll consider the makeup of the committee after we adjourn," said Fred. "If anybody particularly wants to serve on the subcommittee, just let me know. As to the name, that will be up to the Chair."

"But you're the Chair," said Lionel.

"You found me out," conceded Fred.

"Then why didn't you just say, 'The name will be up to me'?"

"One of the privileges of being the Chair is the right to refer to oneself in the third person, as the Chair. And I chose to avail myself of that privilege. It makes it sound less pushy to say that it will be up to the Chair, rather than saying it will be up to me."

"Well, you didn't fool me one bit," said Lionel. "And I think it sounds stilted—the Chair. How would you like me to refer to myself as the Lionel?"

"If you would prefer that, it would be fine with me," said the Chair, and then he adjourned the meeting.

A week later, the Chair called the meeting of the new subcommittee to order.

"Am I mistaken, Fred, or do we have the full Finance Committee membership here?" asked Harvey Holdem.

"No, you're right, Harv. Everyone asked to participate on the subcommittee, so I appointed everyone."

"Then we're not a subcommittee, are we?"

"Yes, I checked the rules and, fortunately, there's nothing that prevents a subcommittee from being composed of the entire committee."

"That's a relief, but this is not likely to help with the interpersonal problem we had at the last meeting, is it?"

"We'll see. It may just be the fact of creating a subcommittee that makes things flow more smoothly, rather than its composition."

"What's our name going to be?" asked Lionel.

"Group Regarding Expenses and Elimination of Deficits, GREED."

"Couldn't we come up with something a little more appealing?"

"I thought it was very descriptive myself," said the Chair. "Now could we please start with ideas for expense reductions?"

"Well, I was looking at last month's computer printout on pencil consumption," said James Freeport, "and I noted that we're up from 2.94 pencils per attorney per month to 3.68. I find that alarming."

"That's peanuts," said Gary Swath.

"No, it's pencils. But now that you mention it, the

printout on peanuts used as snacks in late-afternoon meetings took quite a jump as well."

"I meant that the expense involved in pencils is peanuts," explained Gary. "Our annual pencil expense was only $253.87 last year."

"Yes, but our peanut expense for the year was in the low $400s. In any case, though, it's not the absolute dollars involved, it's the percentage increase. Our pencil consumption jumped about 25%. If that type of increase were experienced in other expense areas, we'd be talking major bucks."

"Okay, then maybe we should do away with peanuts at meetings," said James.

"Wait one little damn minute here, please," said Lionel. "That's the reason I go to meetings: for the peanuts. I'd rather do away with pencils. But I don't think it's necessary to do away with either. I think we could continue both pencils and peanuts at their present level and still effect a major reduction in our expenses."

"Now you're talking, Lionel," said the Chair.

"*The* Lionel, to you."

"Okay, now you're talking, *the* Lionel. But how do you propose to cut expenses and still continue the peanuts and pencils?"

"You travel, don't you?" asked Lionel.

"Of course I do," said the Chair, "but what does that have to do with it?"

"By plane?"

"Yes, by plane."

"Then, being an observant fellow you've no doubt noticed those little packets of peanuts they hand out."

"You're suggesting that we save our packet of peanuts and bring it back to the firm?"

"Not packet, packets. If you ask the flight attendant, you'll always get an extra, sometimes two. And often I find that the people sitting next to me don't eat their peanuts. You can either ask them or, if you're too embarrassed, wait until they get up and go to the bathroom and then snatch them."

"You're serious, aren't you."

"Darn tootin' I am. Here are six packets from my most recent trip to New York," said Lionel, emptying the roasted almonds onto the conference table.

"What if we're hungry, though?" asked Gary. "Can we eat the nuts on the plane?"

"I leave that to your conscience," said Lionel. "But technically, they're firm property."

"I'm almost afraid to ask," said Fawn Plush, "but how do you propose to reduce the pencil expense?"

"Almost every place you go, there are pencils and pens around. And yet I'm sure that our lawyers blithely ignore them. Look at this," said Lionel, opening his briefcase and grabbing a handful of pens and pencils. " 'Harry Block's Insurance Agency,' 'Marriott Hotels,' 'Charles Greene, DDS.' And we go on buying our own. What a waste."

"Even if we could save some money with your idea, the Lionel," said the Chair, "how could we possibly send a memo asking our lawyers to collect peanuts from airlines and writing implements from all over the place. Isn't that a little beneath us?"

"Not if framed properly."

"How would you frame it in a way that wouldn't sound cheap?"

"Simple. Basically, it's an ecological issue. What happens to all of those uneaten peanuts and unused pens and pencils? Eventually they become solid waste, without ever serving their intended use. By making use of them, our firm will be doing its part for the environment—and for our bottom line."

[STANLEY'S NOTE: The month after GREED circulated its memo, per lawyer pencil consumption plummeted to 1.74, and the Lionel was selected Finance Committee Partner of the Month.]

Sentimental Slobbery

Maybe it's unfair to paint lawyers as greedy. Heaven knows, other professions are hardly models of abstinence—even the clergy. Since I never had much of a hankering for holiness, though, I guess I'm stuck writing about us lawyers.

Of course, not all of us are driven by wealth. Some of us could make a whole lot more money in business. And others have chosen to practice law in a way that's never going to make them rich. One of those people is Maggie, my granddaughter.

Maggie is certainly not obsessed with money. In fact, I used to accuse her of being obsessed with poverty. She had the chance to grab the big bucks at a large law firm, but resisted, opting instead to provide legal services to the poor of New York City. As you can see, my influence on her has been limited. But her influence on me . . . that's another story.

It's hard for me to talk about Maggie without sounding like a sentimental slob. And I hate that. But if you've got to be a slob, I suppose you might as well be a sentimental one.

Let me back up first. I pretty much lost touch with Harriet and my daughter, Juliete, after they moved to Los Angeles. If I didn't have time for them when we were living in the same house, I sure wasn't going to chase after them in Lala Land. But I didn't lose touch completely. I called Juliete on her birthday, and sent her birthday and graduation gifts. But my efforts didn't exactly put me in line for Father of the Year.

Out of the blue, though, I got an invitation to Juliete's wedding. I'm not sure what made me decide to attend . . . Oh, yes, that's right; Bertha reminds me that she had something to do with that decision. At any rate, I went. And it was a disaster.

For one thing, Harriet was there. I hadn't seen her since she had left for LA. And she looked terrific, which struck me as a lot of nerve. She was accompanied by her husband, William, who was "in real estate." When I asked what that meant, it turned out that he had inherited six apartment buildings from his papa, which, through William's astute decision to do nothing for twenty years, were now worth a fortune. This allowed him to engage in his favorite pastime, which he described as "playing the ponies." William and I, I realized, would never become close.

On the brighter side, Juliete was even prettier than her mother—reddish hair, high cheekbones and a smile that lit up the room. From the limited time we were able to spend together at the wedding, her personality seemed to match her smile.

Her chosen mate, Knox, however, had two strikes against him. He was from Texas. And, worse, he was a CPA. Knox was in practice with his father, Billy Bob, who wore a string tie and alligator-skin boots to the wedding, which is strike three, four, five or six, depending on how you count.

I'm probably coming across as a closed-minded bigot. We all have certain hot buttons. But these are just first impressions. Sometimes we get beyond them. Would it make any difference to you if you knew that I now own a pair of alligator-skin cowboy boots myself? That's the truth. Gift of Billy Bob. 'Course I don't exactly wear them to the office. But I *am* quite an attraction at the annual firm barbecue.

Anyway, the wedding was something of a disaster. But in retrospect, I think that Juliete and I made a connection there. Maybe we have matching eye twinkles. Whatever it was, she told me she was going to stay in touch. And that she did.

Wasn't more than ten months later I got the call from Juliete telling me I was going to be a grampa. Shocked the hell out of me, I'll tell you. I took Bertha out to lunch to celebrate. And I decided right then and there, at lunch, that I may not have been much of a father, but I was going to be one hell of a grandfather.

About four months later, on my birthday as a matter of fact, my grandson-in-law-the-accountant, Knox, called to say that Margaret Sue had arrived, a healthy 6 lbs, 14 oz, and that mother and child were both doing "jist dandy as all get-out." The joy of having a grandchild was marred only by the thought that Maggie Sue (mercifully, we've managed to drop the Sue) might be blessed with a Texas drawl, just like old Papa Knox.

A few days later, I flew down to Houston to make the personal acquaintance of this Maggie, laden with gifts I'd purchased with Bertha's help. I'm not sure how well we picked, but I'll bet a nickel that Maggie was the only one of her Houston contemporaries who bedded down in Chicago Cubs pajamas. In my unbiased opinion, Maggie was far and away the prettiest of all the little chimps in the nursery.

No one who has not had the experience can possibly appreciate the joy of grandparenting. For most of us, the experience comes at a time when we are all-too-painfully aware of our own mortality, wondering what we will leave behind. And then out of the blue emerges this answer—alive, untarnished, full of possibilities. And we are privileged to participate in this life of possibilities without any of the obligations of parenting (here I speak for others, as

I assumed so few parental obligations myself). Little wonder, then, the strength of the bonds that are forged between grandparents and grandchildren.

I spoiled Maggie rotten, of course, but that's a grandpa's prerogative. I sent her gifts not just on her birthday, but whenever I felt like it, which was often. I watched her reaction to these gifts carefully, though. I didn't want to *buy* my granddaughter's affection. And I was happy to see that I did not. Each gift was a surprise to Maggie. She never came to expect them of me. I tested this once, when she was six, arriving for a visit empty-handed and receiving no less warm a welcome than when I bore an armful of packages.

I was exotic to Maggie, I think. I lived far away. I dressed and looked a bit odd, with my balding pate and bow tie. I was not afraid to be silly (unlike Knox and his father, Billy Bob, who, as accountants, were incapable of silliness). I talked funny, too. ("You speak Northern, Grandpa," Maggie told me at age three. "Can you teach me?")

And Maggie and I developed our "special things," as she called them. I read to her, not from children's books, but from classics like *Tom Sawyer* and even *Don Quixote*. We listened to Gilbert & Sullivan operettas together, and I told her how, in college, I'd played the Lord High Executioner (I cut off her head) and Sir Joseph Porter, KCB (together we polished up the handle of the big front door of her house). When she was old enough to read, I wrote to her once a week (Bertha's favorite task). She came to visit me, and we went to Wrigley Field to watch the Cubs (the high point of my life may well have been the foul ball off the bat of Ron Santo that I caught at that game. I handed the ball to Maggie nonchalantly, as if I snagged one at every game I went to. She has it on her desk at work now, in a plexiglass box.) That same trip, we went to see the doll house at the Museum of Science and Industry (or, as she called it when she was six, "the Museum of Science and Interesting"). There were other visits alone together, and celebrations of our mutual birthday.

Well, maybe you didn't believe me when I said that I get reduced to a sentimental slob. But there you have it, proof positive.

You might wonder how a legal aid lawyer like Maggie would get on with the likes of a big firm partner like me. Truth is, we'd relate darn well even if we weren't related. We respect one another. And we both bring a passion to what we do. Of course, Maggie thinks I waste my passion on the wealthy. And me, I've learned to keep my big mouth shut.

Advice to the Lawlorn

To give lawyers at the firm an outlet for their multitude of problems and frustrations, I started an Advice to the Lawlorn column in our firm newsletter. Below is a sampling of the letters I've received, together with my responses.

Dear Stanley,

It's about time for associate reviews again, and every time they come I get incredibly nervous. Realistically, I should have no problems, I know. My work is good. Clients seem to like me. And I have support from some of the most important partners in the firm. I feel that I should have my feelings under better control by now, since I'm a member of the Executive Committee. Do you have any suggestions?

Nervous

Dear Nervous,

Relax. Your concerns are not unusual, and not nearly as serious as many. Another Executive Committee member wrote to me recently about his fear that he's going to flunk his trigonometry exam.

Dear Stanley,

I am in love with our receptionist. I find myself going in and out of the office all day, just so I can hear her ask, "Going out, Mr. Stack?" or "Out to lunch, Mr. Stack?" Is there anything I can do to make this experience more satisfying? My name is Mr. Flack.

Otto Flack

Dear Otto,

Changing your last name is a simple legal procedure. Many have found this a far easier solution than the more conventional one of trying to train your receptionist to learn your present name. If she doesn't like Flack, Otto, don't give her Flack.

For an excellent treatment of the subject, see the article in 78 Harv. L. Rev. at 569 entitled "Name Changes to Snare Receptionists: A New Approach," by Sheila (formerly Joe) Hopkins. And should things not work out between you and your receptionist, remember: changing your last name back again is a simple legal procedure.

Dear Stanley,

Since I came to the firm several years ago, many of our young associates have disappeared. As you might imagine, this concerns me deeply.

      Frightened

Dear Frightened:

Relax, there is no need to be concerned. Your letter reflects a common misconception. None of our associates has "disappeared." A few have been misplaced, but most of them have left for more lucrative or rewarding positions.

Dear Stanley,

I am a young associate and I am a little confused about the governance of our firm. I know that there are partners and that there is an Executive Committee, but I don't understand what each of them does. Can you explain the relationship between the partnership as a whole and the Executive Committee?

      Curious

Dear Curious,

Of course I can. Our firm is a democracy. The partnership has final authority to decide all matters that come before it. The Executive Committee decides what matters come before the partnership.

Dear Stanley,

I thought your readers would like to hear about some of the situations that we messengers get into. One recent job that sticks out in my mind involved an envelope that I was to deliver to an apartment at midnight one night. As soon as I picked up the envelope, I noticed the pungent smell of perfume emanating from it. The lawyer's initials, S.W.A.K., instead of appearing above the firm name, were on the back of the envelope. As I rode up the elevator in the ritzy Gold Coast apartment building, a romantic old Johnny Mathis tune was being piped through the stereo sound system and the pace of my heartbeat was beginning to quicken. Slowly I floated down the plush hallway carpet and approached the door. I heard the soft strains of Ahmad Jamal wafting through the transom as I grabbed the solid gold knocker and thrust it downward, in a knocking motion. Faint moans could be heard from inside. Suddenly the door flew open and there in front of me, dressed in nothing but a. . . [NOTE: This letter, intended for *Playlawyer*, was sent erroneously to us.]

Dear Stanley:

I've been reading in the papers about how large firms around the country are opening foreign offices, left and right, Tokyo and Tahiti. Do we have any plans to join the crowd abroad?

Internationally Inclined

Dear Internationally:

Our Executive Committee is studying the matter closely. First we surveyed our membership for foreign languages, and found that three of them were fluent in Pig Latin. Not discouraged, though, we've enrolled Percifal Snikkety in a crash Berlitz course in Japanese. He already can ask directions to the nearest sushi bar. In short, it'll be a while (if-ay oo-yay o-knay ut-whay I-ay ean-may).

Dear Stanley:

I'm a new associate at the firm. Around the end of the year, I noticed partners scurrying around the office like crazy, looking at sheets that had a lot of numbers on them and appearing alternately ashen and gleeful. Is this some kind of game? What the heck was going on?

Bewildered

Dear Bewildered:

No, it was not a game. It was deadly serious. All year long, partners at law firms work in order to pay expenses and salaries. Whatever they collect in the last two weeks, though, they get to keep. Partners aren't that smart.

Dear Stanley:

I have read with distress about the continuing problem we have with food and soda disappearing from conference rooms set up to host client meetings. Obviously, a notice in the daily office bulletin is not sufficient to deter the food criminals among us. I suggest that we begin poisoning one sandwich and one drink at each meeting. This should put an end to this dastardly practice.

Outraged

Dear Outraged:

Nice idea, Attila. But who is going to drag the client bodies out when food is *not* stolen?

Dear Stanley:

Could somebody explain to me how the fax machine works?

Teleconfused

Dear Teleconfused:

Of course. I contacted our fax department and they tell me it's very simple. There is a tiny person lying on his back in each machine, with a miniature typewriter. When a document is to be sent, the sending person calls the person in the receiving machine and reads the copy to him. That person then types out the copy at the other end. The reason that our fax charges are so high is that the critters consume an enormous amount of food and beverages for their size.

Dear Stanley:

I'm upset about the firm's smoking policy. I work under a lot of pressure and, frankly, I need a drag now and again. But my department has been designated as non-smoking. I can't smoke on planes, I can't smoke at work. I'm thinking of ending it all.

Smoking-ender

Dear Smoking-ender:

I'm sorry you're so distressed about the firm's smoking policy. Should you be contemplating suicide during work hours, however, I think you should be aware that the Executive Committee has designated certain areas as non-suicide areas. Clint will be circulating a memo soon.

Dear Stanley:

Is the firm considering using recycled paper to show its concern for the environment?

Greenie

Dear Greenie:

As usual, the firm is way ahead of the pack. We've instituted a program that will obviate the need for most recycling altogether. Almost all memos circulated around the firm are repeats of other memos circulated earlier. Henceforth, all memos will be circulated undated, then collected and filed by our newly-hired Director of Repetitive Memos. A person wishing to send a similar memo thereafter will contact the Director, who will locate, re-circulate, re-collect and re-file the memo.

Dear Stanley,

I have a client who is impossible. He calls me at 4 on a Friday to draft a complicated agreement that he says he needs on Monday at 9. I get it to him and then I don't hear from him again for four weeks. He then demands a complete rewrite by the next morning. The deal goes through and he buys two new homes, one in Aspen and one on the Costa del Sol. I send him a bill for two grand and he bitches. Any suggestions?

Still Living in a Studio
Apartment

Dear Still Living,

Ever thought about academia, where clients are just case names and the skies are not cloudy all day? (And your clients live in dorm rooms.)

If the Moccasin Fits, Wear It

I remember going away to camp one summer on the beautiful shores of Lake Mendota, up in Madison, Wisconsin. Camp Indianola. My folks couldn't afford it, but Cutter footed the bill as a reward for my getting all A's in school that year, and getting myself elected president of my class.

Didn't seem like such a momentous couple of months back then—just a good time, with plenty of sports—but it turned out to be one of the greatest growth experiences in my life. Being away from home for the first time, learning to get along with others, finding things I was good at and things I was not so good at, eating new foods (or going hungry), respecting skills that others had and I didn't, pitching in to get things done around the cabin or on a canoe trip, winning, losing—yes, in retrospect, those were mighty important lessons.

It's odd what sticks with you from an experience like that. We had an honor society up at Camp Indianola—the Order of the Silver Moccasins. I can't really remember what exactly you had to do to be inducted into the OSMs. It was only for senior campers, and I was far too young to be considered, in any case. But I sure do remember that it was something special. And I remember the campfire ceremony in which counselors, who were former campers and OSMs themselves, dressed in Indian costume, performed Indian dances and tapped those who were being called as new OSM members. (Actually, "tap" is a colossal misnomer.

The procession of Indians would come to a stop in front of the person to be chosen, the leader would face that person and thump his hands down on both of his shoulders, three times, THUMP, THUMP, THUMP, while at the same time, the drum sounded a jolting BOOM, BOOM, BOOM. I shuddered each time it happened, and thought how I could never become an OSM myself, because I'd collapse from the force of the thumping on my shoulders.) That was almost seventy years ago, so I guess it made an impression on me. And I'm sure that those who belonged to the OSMs felt a strong bond among them.

Partnership used to be something special, too. Oh, there were no THUMP, THUMP, THUMPs or BOOM, BOOM, BOOMs (at least not at our firm), but it meant something. Today, I guess it still means something, but I'm not sure exactly what.

When you joined our law firm, the expectation used to be that you'd stick around, serve your tour of duty and, unless you exposed yourself twice in the reception area or blew the statute of limitations, you'd become a partner. There were exceptions, of course. People *did* screw up. (At the Fairweather firm, weeding people out has never been our strong suit.) And others chose to leave, for a variety of reasons—from teaching law to opening a hardware store. But most people, it seemed, stuck around and grasped the golden ring.

That golden ring wasn't all that it was cracked up to be, of course. The difference in pay might not be all that great. By the time you made your monthly capital contribution, you might wish you were still an associate. And your new pay (unlike your old) wasn't even guaranteed, depending, as it did, on the firm's performance. (It's always seemed a bit bizarre to me that we guarantee the pay of the most recent additions to our firm and leave our partners to collect what's left. A more rational approach would have the partners decide what their take will be, and give the associates what's left over. Now *that* would give the little buggers some incentive to bill a few hours.)

And as a partner, you now had some enormous potential liabilities. We partners used to view those liabilities as vague, theoretical possibilities. In recent years, those vague possibilities have become multi-million-dollar realities for some of my compatriots at other firms. In the future, we're going to see plenty more people turn down the golden ring because of that potential liability, perhaps on advice of counsel.

And besides all of that, once you became partner you were pretty much excluded from all the reliable sources of information that you had developed as an associate. Come to think of it, the main advantages of partnership seem to be a larger office and a speaker phone.

Point is, though, despite all of the drawbacks to partnership, there was the *illusion* of a golden ring. And partners—even those who knew better—seemed to take some pleasure in perpetuating that illusion. So partnership became something a bit mystical, something you wanted for itself, regardless of what the hell it meant.

Twenty-five years ago the main criterion for being elected a partner was, I believe, longevity at the firm. If you were around and still breathing after six years, you were elected. Oh sure, in our partnership meetings we talked about having to be a top-flight lawyer. And to an extent we meant it (some of us meant it much more than others). But when the expectation is that everybody will be admitted, it becomes very difficult to maintain quality. The standard tends to become devalued to the least common denominator. ("Sure Joe is no Justice Brandeis, but he's every bit as good as that idiot Harry in the trusts and estates department.") And before too long, you develop a group of partners who cannot themselves distinguish between really excellent lawyers and journeymen. (And how do you tell some of those people that, if you were applying the standard that you ought to, they wouldn't be partners?)

The main attribute of partnership, back then, was tenure. It was never expressed that way. In theory, the partnership agreement was only for a term of a year (or two or three). But in fact, once you were a partner—unless you did something horrendous—you'd be a partner for life, or at least until mandatory retirement. Fact is, out of loyalty, we even kept on some people who did some pretty horrendous things. And mandatory retirement turned out to be not so mandatory, after all. Take me, for instance.

Now I'm not at all sure that the state of affairs I've described above was sensible or desirable. But during this period—when longevity was the main criterion and tenure the primary attribute—a sense of camaraderie seemed to prevail among our partners. By and large, we trusted and got along with one another. We treated one another with respect or, if that's too strong a word, consideration. Indeed, we even treated associates with consideration (more than a peppercorn, too). Often the reason that marginal candidates were elected partners was out of concern for them as individuals.

Things have changed. Longevity won't get you into our partnership anymore. And once in, it's no longer "until death (or sometimes, mandatory retirement) do us part." We're defrocking partners almost as fast as we're frocking them. By themselves, I don't think that either of these changes is necessarily bad. What they seem to have brought along with them, however, is.

The bottom line. What I think it comes down to is the bottom line. Law firm partnerships have become business relationships (which they always were) and nothing else (which they once were). Even that wouldn't be so bad if we were better business people, if, for example, we recognized (as most of our corporate counterparts do) that we ought to reward people for teaching others, penalize them for being impossible to work with, etc.

There's nothing very mystical about partnership anymore. Now, of course, I'll grant you that business is plenty important. Without it, the firm would not survive. But the challenge we law firms face is how to maintain our business equilibrium without letting that equilibrium tip us over. (I rather like that: equilibrium tipping you over.) What we need, I think, is a way to instill the THUMP, THUMP, THUMPs and BOOM, BOOM, BOOMs into our law firms.

Listen, Buddy *or* The Quality of Life Is Strained, It Droppeth...

We at the Fairweather firm listen. In fact, we have created so many committees designed to listen to our attorneys' problems—committees on morale, on training, on health, on associate retention, on family—that it is sometimes difficult to know which of these committees to turn to. This has led to occasional jurisdictional disputes between committees and, worse, to a nagging fear that an issue relating to the welfare of lawyers at the firm might (unintentionally, of course) slip between the cracks, unattended. To exorcise this troublesome possibility, the Executive Committee constituted the chairs of the four committees that deal with these welfare issues an ad hoc task force on quality of life. What follows is a transcript of the first meeting of that task force.

"Now as I understand it, we're charged with figuring out a way to assure that none of our attorneys' problems go unattended," said Ruth Tender. "Why don't we start by seeing whether there are any common elements to the problems our committees are dealing with. What are you finding, Frank?"

"Well, we on the Committee on Associate Morale deal with a wide range of problems, but I'd say that most of them involve the feeling among associates that nobody is listening to their concerns," said Franklin Goodtime.

"That's pretty much the case with us on the Family Focus Committee," said Ruth. "What about you, Steve?"

"I'd say that our situation is a little different on the Committee on Associate Retention and Evaluation. Some associates complain that we're not listening to their concerns, but more complain that we're not doing anything about them."

"I agree with Steve. At the Committee on Health in Practice we're always getting the complaint that nothing is happening," said Rip Winkle.

"I'm surprised to hear that, Rip. Those who come to us at Associate Morale *assume* that nothing is going to happen; that's a given," said Frank.

"In any case, it seems that we have two basic threads," said Ruth. "One suggests that our committees are not listening and the other that we may be listening, but we're not doing anything."

"It seems to me that we're doing pretty darn well, then," said Steve.

"What do you mean, pretty well?" asked Ruth.

"We only have two problems. Most of the other committees have a lot more problems than that," answered Steve.

"But it's not just the number of problems, it's their seriousness. And ours are pretty basic," said Ruth.

"I think we can solve them if we take them one at a time," offered Frank.

"One at a time sounds okay to me," said Rip.

"Count me in on that approach," said Steve.

"No objection here," added Ruth. "Which shall we tackle first?"

"Way I see it is we've got the doing problem and the listening problem," said Frank. "The doing problem is toughest, so I think we ought to address that one first. Any ideas?"

"We could deny that we're not doing anything, point to all of our accomplishments," suggested Rip.

"Such as?" asked Steve.

"Well, we on CHIP have succeeded in ordering some firm T-shirts for use in sporting activities," said Rip.

"Dynamite," said Steve. "How can anybody complain about the quality of life at the firm now that we have our own T-shirts?"

"I can't understand that myself," said Rip. "But we have had a few complaints, nonetheless."

"Such as?" asked Steve.

"Well, some people have objected to the pink and green color of our T-shirts. And others have objected to the fact that we have only mediums. And finally, some think that the $9.95 price tag is a little hefty."

"You're kidding; we charge for them?"

"I tried to get the Finance Committee to foot the bill, but they just laughed."

"Well, I think that we on the Committee on Associate Morale have accomplished a bit more than that," said Frank. "Recently, several associates complained to us that they didn't get any sense of how the firm was doing financially, except through reading the legal press."

"So what did you do?" asked Ruth.

"We agreed to circulate the same information to them that the Executive Committee circulates to all partners in the firm."

"But that's garbage. All it ever says is 'Receivables are 10% above budget, but income is 15% below budget. Payables are close to projections. If we all bill the work in progress within the next thirty days and collect the fees at the rate we projected, we should be on or close to budget;

otherwise, sell the dog.' That can't have satisfied our associates, since it doesn't satisfy any of our partners."

"You're right, Ruth. I guess we really can't argue that we did something," agreed Frank. "But maybe we can answer the doing problem by saying that in a firm this size, with as many committees as we have, it's impossible to accomplish anything—so they shouldn't expect it."

"The older associates know that, but the younger associates will never buy it," said Steve. "I have another approach to solving the doing problem that I think will put it to rest for good."

"What's that?" asked Ruth.

"Simple. Remember what our Committee on Associate Retention and Evaluation did when the associates complained that our review procedure was unfair?"

"No, refresh our recollections."

"We devised a form that required associates to provide detailed information about the nature of every project they'd worked on in the last year, exactly what they'd done, how much time they'd spent on each aspect of the work, how they assessed their performance on each aspect and how they thought they'd benefited from the project. Then prior to the evaluation process, we required that they give an oral presentation on all of this to a committee of three partners, headed by Nails Nuttree. Midway through the first review period under the new system, the associates came to us and begged us to return to the old unfair system."

"But how will that help us with the doing problem?" asked Ruth.

"We just tell them about this and give them a few more examples of what our committees do when they do do something, and the associates will realize that the last thing they want is for any committee to do anything at all."

"Brilliant, Steve, that ought to solve the doing problem, all right. But what do we do about the listening problem?"

"That one's a bit tougher, I'm afraid. The reason none of our partners listen is that we're all so sick of hearing the same complaining and whining year after year that we've lost our ability to listen. Besides, listening is expensive. It takes an enormous amount of our partners' time."

"Wait a minute," said Frank. "I think I know how to accomplish the listening without using any partner time."

"How in the world are you going to do that?" asked Steve.

"Our associates want senior people to listen to their problems, right?"

"Right."

"But none of our senior people work with associates anymore, so none of the associates even know what our senior people look like, right?"

"Right, but so what?"

"So what? We go out and hire a number of senior citizens who are retired—the way that all of our senior partners (except Stanley) should be—to play the roles of concerned senior partners. These senior citizens have nothing to do, and they've never heard the complaints of our associates before, so for them it won't be such a problem to sit and listen. We pay them a few bucks (they won't want much or they'll lose their social security benefits) and, boom, we've solved our listening problem."

"Sounds good, Frank, but there's still one problem. These senior citizens we hire aren't going to know beans about the complaints our associates bring in, so how are they going to respond to them?"

"Respond? Who needs to respond? All they're supposed to do is *listen*. We train them to nod their heads, say 'uh-huh,' 'I see' and 'is that so,' and we've solved our listening problem."

"Good work, gentlemen. Looks like we've solved our quality of life problem in one meeting," said Ruth. "I move we adjourn."

Playing Lawyer

For years, as I've said, when Maggie was much younger, I wrote to her most every week. Bertha reminded me recently that I kept copies of those letters. (We lawyers make multiple copies of everything—letters, drafts of documents, final versions of documents, memos, you name it. And we save them forever, for fear of . . . for fear of . . . for fear. Heaven only knows what is buried in our files. And chances are that only heaven *will* know, since nobody down here on earth is ever likely to look back at those files.)

Bertha suggested that I include one of my letters to Maggie in this book. At first, the idea did not appeal to me. The letters were rather personal. But Bertha persisted (not unusual for her, when she thinks she's right) and presented several letters for my perusal. With Maggie's permission (indeed, to her great pleasure) I'm sharing the one below, which I wrote on May 8, 1968.

My Dear Maggie Dumpling:

Thank you so much for the lovely drawings that you sent with your last letter. One is hanging in my office (the picture of the choo-choo train) and the other is taped to my refrigerator at home. I would have put them both up in my office, except that I was afraid that your tiger was so fierce-looking it would frighten some of the people who visit me at the office.

You asked me in your last letter what I do. That's a difficult question, and one that requires a pretty long answer, I'm afraid. It may be rather hard to explain to you.

Nonetheless, I'm glad that you are interested enough to ask, and so I will try to answer as best I can. If you do not understand something, please ask me about it in your next letter.

What I do most is try to help people solve their problems. Let me try to give you some examples. Do you remember the last time I was in town, you had a big argument with your friend next door, Jamie I think his name is? You both thought that the frisbee you were playing with was yours. When I came along, you were quite angry and were starting to fight. Then we discussed it and came to the agreement that, since you both had identical frisbees and one of them was missing and we couldn't tell which one, you and Jamie would share this one until the missing one turned up. Neither of you was too happy with that, but it was better than a fight (especially since Jamie is quite a bit bigger than you).

Well, grown-ups have disagreements, too, all the time (though usually not about frisbees). And it wouldn't be a good idea for all of those arguments to wind up in fights. (Just think of all those adults walking around with black eyes.) So we have a system for settling those arguments peacefully: the two people who disagree find lawyers to argue their cases for them, and a person who wears a black robe (like the judge in *Trial by Jury*, but without the wig) decides what to do. So, in one sense, I guess I'm a fulltime arguer. And I get paid by people to argue for them. (I bet you'd like to do that, wouldn't you.) Most of the time, when it's all over, the people I work with aren't a whole lot happier than you and Jamie were about splitting the frisbee.

Here's another example. Remember the night you wanted to stay up real late, to watch *The Wizard of Oz* on television? And your mom and dad told you it was too late. At first you cried, but that didn't work. So then you said you'd be good forever and never ask for anything again in your whole life, ever, if they'd let you stay up. But your mom and dad didn't quite believe that. So, instead, you said you'd get all ready for bed, brush your teeth during a commercial and then promise to go right to sleep, without a story. And you agreed that, the next day, you'd take an afternoon nap and then help Mom set the table for dinner.

You were doing what's called negotiating—offering to give up something in order to get something you wanted. And the agreement you and your mom reached is called a contract. Grandpa spends a lot of his time helping other people get to stay up late or get something else they want.

Maybe I can give you just one more example. Remember that really hot day when you and Jamie decided it would be a good idea to set up a lemonade stand? You had a whole bunch of things that you had to decide—where to put the stand; how much to charge; who would provide the lemonade, the glasses, the sugar; how you and Jamie would split up the profits; who would make the signs; how long you would be open for business; whether you would let other kids join you; and plenty of other things, too. You and Jamie talked about all of those things and decided them yourselves. Well, when big people set up businesses, they have many of the same questions. And sometimes those people need help deciding how they're going to solve their business problems. Your grandpa spends a lot of his time helping them set up their lemonade stands and other businesses.

So, like Sir Joseph Porter KCB in *HMS Pinafore*, I am a lawyer. I don't expect that I'll ever be made the ruler of the Queen's navy, though.

Well, Maggie Dumpling, I hope that gives you some better idea of what your grandpa does. Please write and tell me what you think about all this. Say hello to your mom and dad for me.

> Love and lots of mushy kisses

I had Maggie's response framed and, for years, it hung in my office. I gave it to Maggie for her law school graduation, so now it's up in hers. It reads:

Dear Grandpa Dumpling:
Thanks for telling me what you do. I never knew that you and me do the same thing. But why do people pay you to do it? I want to be an arguer when I grow up.

> Love, but no mushy kisses

Why *do* people pay me to do it? Sometimes, when I'm having a ball practicing law, I've thought that I would do it gladly for nothing. At other times, I've thought that nobody could ever pay me enough.

Rereading my letter to Maggie, I've wondered why so few kids grow up dreaming of becoming a lawyer. Why do kids all play doctor and never play lawyer (even though, as my letter suggests, they're playing lawyer all the time, without ever recognizing it)? Instead, they are doctors with tiny stethoscopes, firemen with bright red fire engines, cowboys with guns, and astronauts with spaceships. Maybe what we need are miniature briefcases, dictating machines and legal pads, so that more kids can grow up playing lawyer.

At any rate, Maggie fulfilled her dream. She's become an arguer, and a damn good one, too. And I think I may have had a little something to do with her decision.

Aiding Legal Aid

Maggie and I talk a lot. In fact, I've shared so many of my experiences with Maggie that she tells me she feels as if she's been a partner at my firm as long as I have (which she thinks is much too long). Maggie seems to have the same appreciation her grampa does for the absurdity of many of the things we do at the Fairweather firm. And the more I speak with Maggie about her legal aid experience, the more I learn about how we large law firms are viewed by the rest of the world (and the more I'm struck by some of the similarities between the way Maggie's and my offices run). So that I can show you what I mean, Maggie has given me permission to share with you these minutes of a recent meeting of her legal aid attorneys.

The meeting was called to order by Maggie Blylock, who announced that there were two principal items for discussion: funding of the office for the coming year and staffing of the new major case that the office had undertaken, *Strauss* v. *City of New York*. She called on treasurer Fred Gluck to deliver his financial report.

"The office has a bank balance of $20,439.84," announced Fred.

"Positive or negative?" asked Laurie Minnow.

"Positive," answered Fred.

"That's incredible," said Gary Traurig. "I don't think we've ever been that much in the black. I think we should commend our treasurer and give ourselves $125 a month raises, retroactive to January of last year."

"Not so fast, Gary," said Maggie. "I talked to Fred before the meeting and I think he'd better tell us more about how he's achieved our bank balance."

"We have achieved the balance through more aggressive cash management techniques," announced Fred.

"What the hell does that mean?" asked Cecelia Brooks-Trout.

"Basically, we haven't paid any of our bills in the last ninety days," said Fred.

"And if we had, what would the balance be?" asked Laurie.

"On a pro forma basis, factoring in payment of all outstanding accounts payable, that would leave us with a balance of $2,319.23, negative."

"That's still not so bad," said Gary.

"How do you figure that?" asked Cecelia.

"Well, when you look at the federal deficit, our two grand looks like peanuts."

"That may be, Gary. But unlike the federal government, our office does not have the power to print money," Maggie observed.

"But our annual law-firm fund-raising effort is about to start, so soon we'll have lots of cash, won't we?" asked Laurie.

"I'm not so sure," said Maggie. "I'm getting some vibes that this may be a tough year for us to hit up some of the firms, because their profits have dropped."

"You mean average per-partner profits have dropped from $500,000 to $475,000? That doesn't exactly put them below the poverty level," said Laurie.

"You'd never know it from talking to them, though," said Maggie. "One of the partners at a major contributing firm was moaning to me about how he'd wanted to buy his daughter Sheila a BMW for high-school graduation, but now he thought she was going to have to settle for a Lexus."

"Poor Sheila. The kid will probably be scarred for life. Imagine, having to show up your first year at Princeton with a Lexus. Yuck," said Gary.

"Even if the firms do continue to support us at the rate they have in the past, we're going to take a hit. They've been contributing $100 per lawyer, and their head count is going to be down quite a bit this year," said Maggie.

"Why don't we try a new gauge? Instead of $100 per lawyer, we'll just ask for a contribution equal to one hour of each lawyer's time, at each lawyer's lowest current billing rate. I'll bet that would double our take," said Fred.

"I'm not so sure," said Gary. "The way some corporations are pounding away at those hourly rates, we might not do so well. And worse, we'd probably get stuck with some contingent contributions."

"Seems to me we should just continue to operate on the same financial basis we always have," suggested Cecelia.

"And what's that?" asked Gary.

"Spend whatever we have to, and pray a lot."

"Well, I suppose there's not too much we can actually do about the financial situation now, anyway," said Maggie. "I just wanted you all to be aware of it. I think we should move on to staffing of *Strauss* v. *State of New York*. You all recall that in *Strauss* we are suing the State, claiming that all of the banking, insurance, housing and transportation laws are unconstitutional because they discriminate against women, minorities, Buddhists and people under 5'6" in height. This obviously is going to require more resources than our office can muster, so our law firm liaison, Cecelia, has been exploring getting help from some of our cooperating law firms. How about telling us where we stand with those firms, Cecelia?"

"In a word, alone."

"What do you mean alone? How did that happen?" asked Laurie.

"Well, first we approached several law firms and told them that we had this sexy new case we were working on that would look real good to law students as part of the firm's pro bono work."

"That should have gotten a good response."

"It did. Except the firms we talked to all found out that other firms had also been asked to participate in this sexy pro bono case, and so they started lobbying me to drop the other firms. I told them that I couldn't do that and assured them that there would be plenty of work for all of them."

"Did that satisfy them?"

"No, they started jockeying for the position of lead counsel."

"But at least it sounds like you have plenty of support lined up," said Fred.

"I did, until they found out what the suit was all about."

"And then what happened?"

"They all managed to develop conflicts of interest or potential conflicts of interest. They all seem to represent a bank or an insurance company or a railroad or a tall person or something."

"But this must happen to these firms all the time. What if a paying client had wanted them to bring a suit like this?" asked Laurie.

"Well, in that case some of these potential conflicts have a way of resolving themselves, or disappearing like magic," said Cecelia.

"That's terrible, what are we going to do?" asked Gary.

"Actually, it's not so terrible. When firms take on a pro bono case like this, they tend to put their least experienced attorneys on the matter. So we may gain the prestige of a big firm behind us, but we have the expertise of total novices. I've found a way of getting the best of the big firm experience behind us."

"But I thought you said that all of the large firms had conflicts and couldn't represent us?"

"That's right. But I went to Citizen Action Law Associates, the public interest law firm. And they're composed of some of the best former associates and partners from large firms, those who could no longer take the grind of those firms and decided to go back to what attracted them to law in the first place—the opportunity to achieve social justice. CALA found no conflict in taking on this matter jointly with us. And they didn't care who's billed as lead attorney, either."

Have I Got a Firm for You!

I have a tough time understanding all of the hullabaloo about marketing in law firms. It's as if we never marketed before.

Lawyers who complain about the need to market sound to me like they're saying this: "Imagine *us*, those called to the Bar, having to dirty our hands by selling. Why, the shame of it all!" And if they sound like that to *me*, just imagine what they sound like to clients who have been forced to dirty their own hands selling all their lives.

Of course, selling and marketing aren't the same thing at all. You've got to market before you can sell. To market, you have to analyze your strengths and weaknesses, do the same with your competition, assess where the legal market is going, determine what your niche is going to be, figure out how to portray yourself to the market, etcetera. Now, it doesn't seem to me that this process ought to scare lawyers in the least. In fact, isn't it mighty darn close to what good lawyers are doing in their practice all the time?

And selling, hell, life is selling. Precious few places you can make your mark in this world without an ability to sell. Now how you go about that selling, of course, is a very individual thing.

I got my first real taste of selling one summer, during college. I took a job peddling encyclopedias door to door. Just picked myself out a street each day, knocked on the doors and said, "How would you like to buy a couple hundred dollars worth of books?" Now *that's* a character builder for you.

Of course, you didn't go about it exactly that way. The company I worked for had a pitch all worked out. As I recall it, there were a couple keys to success. First, you had to get in the door. Then, you had to determine whether the person you were talking to was the real decisionmaker. Next, you had to figure out just how interested they were in your product, because you didn't want to waste a whole lot of time with people who weren't going to buy. And finally, if all of those other things fell into place, you had to be able to close the sale.

As I recall, my company had an interesting approach to selling. Once we determined that the client—I mean potential customer . . . Now, that's a slip laden with meaning. Treating potential customers as if they were clients may well be the key to making them clients. And while we're at it, did you know that Webster's first definition of client is "a person under the protection of another?" Think about that one a bit. Anyway, once the potential customer was found to be a good prospect, we carpeted the person's living room with large vinyl pictures of the encyclopedias, of a free bookcase, and of a Bible and several other giveaways that I can't now recall. I think the theory was that the customer would be so glad to reclaim the space occupied by all of our pictures that he would buy our product. I sometimes wonder whether we in law firms may not be operating under a similar theory now, what with all of the brochures, newsletters and surveys we are distributing to potential clients. Maybe we ought to offer them a deal—we'll stop sending them all that crap if they hire us.

I said the experience of selling encyclopedias was character building, and it was. I had an awful lot of doors slammed in my face. And I spent countless hours talking to people who it later turned out were not at all interested in what I had to offer. I developed a healthy appreciation for luck and timing the day I sold a set of books to a couple who had just that week learned that dear old Aunt Gladys had gone to her eternal reward, and left them a reward as well. (Can you believe I still remember that name? Strange things, minds.)

But I also learned the value of creativity in selling. One day, I encountered two families just three doors apart, both of whom seemed genuinely interested in an encyclopedia, but said that they couldn't swing the purchase price. I asked the second family if they knew their neighbors, let's call them the Smiths. Know them, I was told; they were great friends, the kids were inseparable. Then how about inviting the Smiths over for a soft drink, I suggested . . . yes, right now, I knew they were home. Might well have been the first joint tenancy in encyclopedias in the company's history. But both families were sure happy. And you know that I was.

On bad days I sometimes wish I was still out peddling encyclopedias, instead of law firms. For one thing, their virtues are a lot easier to describe. For another, they're a whole lot cheaper. And you have something solid to leave behind—a handsome set of books, and maybe even a bookcase and Bible, to boot. Another thing, my encyclopedia customers never called me at home, or complained about the bill.

On better days, though, I don't mind selling my firm. Hell, I built the thing, so I oughta be able to tout it. Fact is, I can work up some pretty good pride in the place, once I start to talking.

One time I recall going out to see the president of a company that made kitty litter, you know, the stuff that cats do their stuff in. Well I'd been introduced to this fellow through a mutual friend, and told that he was looking for counsel for a public offering of his company's stock.

I don't know beans about cats. Don't like them, if you want to know the truth. But I figured I'd better brush up on my felines before making this call. So I took five or six books out of the library and by the time of our meeting I was an expert on everything from Angoras and Mantese to alleys. About ten minutes into our meeting, I started spouting some of my new-found knowledge. But he interrupted me to say that he didn't give a damn what I knew about cats, he wanted to know what my law firm knew about the law. An hour later, he was begging me to get back to cats. We got the legal business, though, and I've been representing them ever since.

So I've never much minded selling my firm. I'm getting a little bit old to be out ringing doorbells, anyway.

Of course, all of this selling stuff takes time, and money. You don't make rain without an expense account. In fact, each of our partners now has an account for client entertainment. And our firm administrator, Clint Hargraves, bugs the hell out of me when we're not spending enough out of that account.

But entertainment has never been my primary sales tool. No, my primary tools have been respect for my client, concern for what the client wanted to accomplish, and asking advice (if you don't think asking somebody for their advice—on anything—is a sales tool, try it some time). Those tools aren't very expensive.

And when I do entertain, like as not I'll have clients over for dinner and cook for them myself. Makes me stand out a bit. Damn few of my competitors are cooking for their clients. I'll stack up my chicken fricassee and a fine bottle of Sauvignon blanc against the best damn marketing brochure in the world.

Ballyhooing the Firm

Like most firms, ours has plunged headlong into the new marketing craze. Here is a partial transcript of the meeting of our Committee on Marketing Efforts (COME), called to consider the recommendations of our new marketing director, Fricka Escher.

"I don't know about this brochure, Fricka. It seems a little flashy to me," said COME Chair, Seymour Plain.

"Not really," replied Fricka. "I looked at what other firms have done and this is pretty tame by comparison."

"Tame?!" exclaimed Rudolph Grossbladt, senior member of the committee. "Why look at it, it's . . . it's . . . printed . . . and, the cover, it's colored . . . scarlet."

"Take it easy, Rudy. Printing is common. And it's not scarlet, it's more carnelian or stammel, actually quite dignified," opined Alphonse Proust.

"Dignified, hogfeathers. Why, when I started practicing . . ."

"Rudy, c'mon now. When you were appointed to the committee, it was on the condition that you never use the phrase, 'when I started practicing,' " Seymour reminded him.

"I know, but I can't help it. But . . . oh, never mind."

"Don't you think we ought to have a few pictures?" asked Harriet Akers. "I mean to spruce it up, give it a little pizazz."

"Pizazz? Pictures?! You don't mean photographs, do you?" asked Rudy, incredulous.

"Yes, many firms use photographs," replied Fricka. "I considered it, but thought that, for our first try, we should go a little more conservative."

"Conservative? Look at this language. Poor drafting. Just listen, here you say, 'Fairweather services all of its clients' needs, from soup to nuts.' Since when did we start serving soup and nuts? What are we, a restaurant? I've marked that up to read—Fricka, take this down—'The departments of the law firm of Fairweather, Winters & Sommers include, without limiting the generality of the foregoing:' And then I list all of our departments, in alphabetical order."

"Rudy, that's dreadful," said Harriet. "It sounds like a trust indenture. We need something that will grab non-lawyers, like what Fricka's written."

"I tend to agree with you," said Herbert Gander, "but I don't like what she's written about the corporate department."

"No, and I think our litigation section needs to be expanded (corporate's description is eighty-two words longer) and moved up closer to the front of the brochure. And I have a thought as to how we can expand it—that injunction I won for Carefree Corporation last week deserves at least a paragraph or two," offered Alphonse.

"But if we have each person rewrite this thing to suit the special interests of his department, we'll never get this thing approved," said Fricka, close to tears.

"Fricka, m'dear, we are a highly democratic firm," cautioned Rudy.

"Well, in drafting brochures democracy sucks . . . I mean, is highly overrated," said Fricka.

"I'd say it's overrated altogether," said Sheldon Horvitz, "but I don't want to wade into the murky waters of politics."

"How about this proposal for a series of seminars for

clients?" asked Seymour, changing the subject. "Can we at least agree on that?"

"Sounds good to me," said Harriet. "How about a date?"

"Love to, Harriet, but I'm afraid I'm married," replied Seymour. "How long have you been holding this candle for me, anyway?"

"You know very well what I meant. When should we hold the first seminar."

"Well, let me see, I'm outa town the first two weeks of next month," said Rudy.

"We're not really going to check everyone's calendar on this, are we?" pleaded Fricka.

"Well, I should think we'd want the entire committee present, in any case," said Rudy.

"Not necessarily. The more people we have, the higher the food bill will be," pointed out Harriet.

"That's right, what *are* we going to serve at the seminar?" asked Alphonse.

"How about soup and nuts, that's what the brochure says we serve," offered Rudy.

"I'm serious," said Alphonse.

"How about a chocolate fondue? That would be unusual. And I happen to love it," suggested Sheldon.

"Will we offer hard liquor?" asked Harriet.

"No, our clients will be stumbling all around the damn conference room," objected Seymour.

"And some of our partners don't hold their booze all that well, either," Herbert reminded the group.

"Which seminar would we do first?" asked Rudy. "Personally, I think something on charitable remainder trusts would be a dynamite kickoff. And I happen to have a speech I delivered in '68 that practically brought the house down at the Remainder Trust Subcommittee of the bar association. I could have a couple of our associates update it in a jiffy."

"I would think something in corporate would be of more general interest—and I *am* vice-chair elect of the city bar committee on corporate law," said Herb.

"Funny, I was thinking that a litigation topic would be just the thing to get the series off with a bang," said Alphonse.

"Why not something on one of our pro bono cases?" suggested Sheldon.

"I'm resigning," announced Fricka.

"Resigning? But we just hired you," said Seymour. "Why in the world would you resign?"

"I accepted this position because I thought the firm was ready to move into the marketing arena. Mr. Fairweather assured me of that in our interview. Now I see that we're going to spend hours putting everything I write into the passive tense and arguing over dates and menus. I think you've hired the wrong person," said Fricka.

"Rome wasn't built in a day," Rudy reminded the former marketing director.

"Neither was Topeka, where I hail from," added Sheldon.

Just then, Stanley Fairweather, who, as managing partner, is an ex-officio member of all firm committees, walked into the room. "Fricka, you're crying. Why the tears?"

"She's resigned," announced Rudy.

"Resigned? That's impossible! Not when we're off to such a good start," said Stanley.

"I'm afraid we're not off to such a good start," said Fricka. "We've been arguing about the content of the brochure, the dates and topics of the seminars, even what food will be served."

"No need for that," said Stanley. "Brochure looks good

to me. I'd like a little more pizazz, a few pictures, but this is a start, so I've sent it off to the printer. And they've assured me they'll have it ready for our first client seminar, two weeks from Tuesday. I'll be speaking on contract negotiations. I think our clients will like the hors d'oeuvres and wines I've selected."

"I unresign," said Fricka.

"Can she do that, technically? Unresign?" asked Rudy.

"We're in a whole new world here, Rudy. Marketing, unresigning . . . you and I are just going to have to adjust, okay?" said Stanley, and he adjourned the meeting.

Oxy and Other Morons

The organized bar is an oxymoron. Maybe that's inevitable, given its diversity. And, quite probably, it's good. Heaven help us all if the bar ever really got organized around issues it wanted to pursue.

In another sense, though, the bar is organized to the hilt. Anyone who thinks our firm has too many committees would think that bar associations are infested with them. Those folks may have invented the committee. Yes, come to think of it, the first committee probably was formed by the ABA—the Athenian Bar Association.

Somebody who's been around as long as I have hasn't avoided run-ins with the bar. To be honest, there was a time when I got rather involved, at the suggestion of some of my partners. They thought that if I became president of the bar—and they meant the American Bar Association, the granddaddy of them all (do you suppose that granddaddy is the only word in the dictionary with four D's? I'll bet it's at least the only one that has D's as four of five consecutive letters), I'd be able to generate a bunch of legal work for the firm.

Well, in the byzantine world of the ABA, you've got to work your way up through the ranks. You become chair of some local bar committee on something or another, you shimmy your way up to president of that bar, you get selected for the ABA House of Delegates, you work through one of the sections at the ABA or the Conference of Bar Presidents or the State Delegates, I'm not sure, it's been too long . . . I lost interest long before the string was played out. But I did manage to serve a two-year stint in

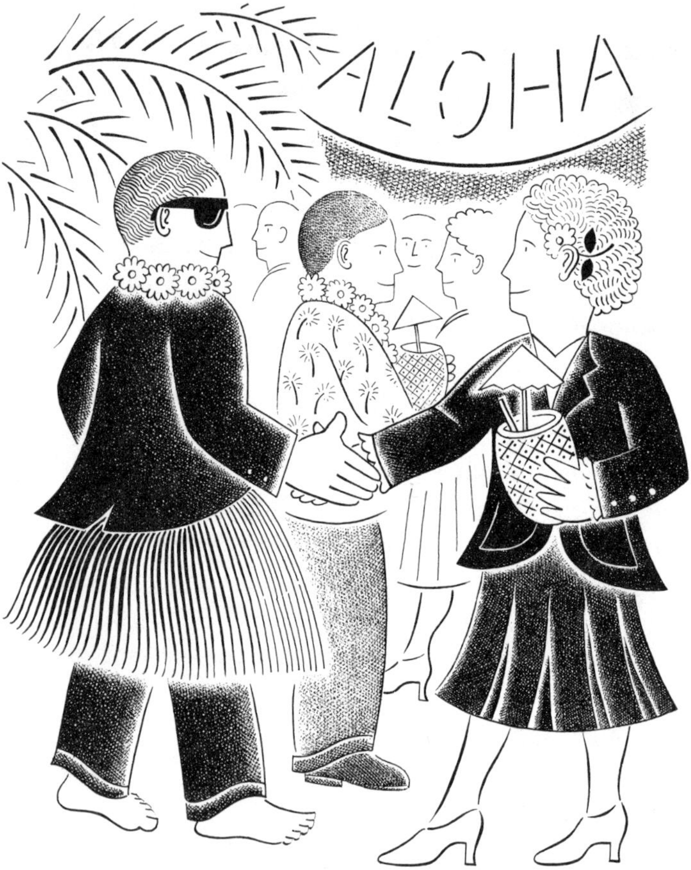
ALOHA

the American Bar Association's House of Delegates, many years ago.

I remember my first meeting vividly. It was in Hawaii in August, and the ABA headquarters hotel was the humongous Sheraton Waikiki. After the long trip there, I collapsed in my room. The next morning I woke up and walked down into the lobby, where I gazed upon a sea of lawyers, all wearing aloha shirts, ABA name tags pinned on their suit coats, and pink and turquoise leis around their necks, and holding aloft Mimosas with multi-colored paper umbrellas stuck into floating pineapple chunks. You've never seen anything so silly-looking. I remember actually shaking my head in disbelief at that surrealistic picture.

The meeting itself began with the introduction of new members of the House of Delegates, who stood, and a reading of the names of those members who had died since the last meeting, who did not stand. Anybody who wanted to speak had to fill out a salmon-colored slip and had to abide by the green, yellow and red lights on the podium that signaled the time remaining to speakers. This is true. I am not making this up.

As I recall, the hottest debate at that meeting centered on a proposal by the Committee on Scope and Correlation (the grim reaper of the ABA) to disband the Admiralty and Maritime Law Committee. The latter fought valiantly and successfully for its life. Indeed, the only time I was lobbied during the meeting was by a Louisiana delegate asking me to "vote with us on this Maritime thing." The clincher in the debate came when a delegate estimated that the cost of keeping the committee in existence for another year was probably less than the cost of the liquor spilled at the ABA president's lavish reception the night before. That clinched my vote.

The other ABA meeting I attended was no less

memorable—in New Orleans in August. (The ABA meetings department has a marvelous sense of humor, scheduling meetings in Chicago in February and in New Orleans in August.) Both the temperature and the humidity hovered around the 100-degree level the whole time I was there, dropping into the low 90s in the evening. Instead of a sea of name tags on aloha shirts, this time I saw those name tags weaving perilously down Bourbon Street every evening. The priorities of that meeting are perhaps best summed up by noting that the House spent twenty minutes debating a proposal to limit the constitutional jurisdiction of the federal courts, but allotted an hour and a quarter to consideration of a proposal to allow law office administrators to become associate members of the ABA. While the level of debate in the House was often quite high, my overall impression comports with Gilbert's lyrics about another House in *Iolanthe*:

> *The House of Peers,*
> *throughout the war,*
> *did nothing in par-tic-u-lar*
> *and did it very well.*

After those two House of Delegate meetings, I aborted my fledgling campaign to become president of the bar. My heart was never in it. You might think that somebody as nimble as I in dealing with all of the committees in my firm would have a field day in the ABA. Not so. At my firm, at least, the committees exist to further the institution; at the ABA, they *are* the institution. And that's too much of a committee-ment for me.

Maybe all of this is sour grapes, the rationalizations of a jilted suitor. I suppose that two years of traveling around the country, first as president-elect and then as president, might have proved interesting. But I've never been one to crave the public spotlight. True, I might have made a lot of valuable contacts. But after two years away from the helm, I'm not sure what would have been left of my beloved firm.

At any rate, all that's left of my campaign now are a couple of boxes of "Fairweather for ABA President" bumper stickers, the brainchild of our Committee on Bar-Related Activities.

Bar Hopping

The Fairweather, Winters & Sommers Committee on Bar-Related Activities (COBRA) is composed of seven members—Chairman Garrison Phelps, his first through fourth vice chairmen, the immediate past chairman, and the past immediate past chairman. Its purpose is to generate business for the firm through active involvement in bar activities and, incidentally, to fulfill the firm's obligations to the legal profession.

Unlike other firm committees that meet in or near the FWS offices, COBRA meets at locations around the country and, sometimes, around the world. The committee's mid-year meeting last February was held in Fairbanks, Alaska.

Each member wore a tag bearing the member's name, city of maternal grandmother's origin, and law board score. The tags were adorned with stripes of various colors to denote past, current or future bar association presidencies, stars to show outstanding attendance records, and ribbons to recognize excellence of performance in last evening's bowlathon. A tiny spotlight was fastened to each tag for night meetings.

The United States Marine Band, towed in on dogsled by an honor guard of huskies, kicked off the opening ceremony with a rendering of "Baby, It's Cold Outside" that brought tears to the eyes of some of the more emotional committee members. Committee members then bowed their heads as clergy of fourteen sects and one devout atheist spread their blessings upon them.

Next, the mayor of Fairbanks presented a key to the city to Chairman Phelps, who promptly misplaced it. The presidents of the Alaska and Fairbanks bar associations each delivered welcoming remarks and proclaimed the committee honorary members of their bar association, for the day.

After a break for lunch, the roll was called and the reading of the minutes of the last meeting was dispensed with by a 4-3 vote. Third Vice Chairman Sylvia Wurrier asked if she might raise a procedural question.

Chairman Phelps noted that nobody had ever asked before whether they could raise a procedural question. They had just gone ahead and raised it. In fact, a recent study done by the Committee on Bar-Related Activities Foundation showed that the percentage of procedural questions dealt with by COBRA had increased from 50 percent in 1981 to more than 64 percent in 1991. Since Sylvia had raised the matter, however, Chairman Phelps said that the committee could consider it.

Past Immediate Past Chairman Percifal Snikkety questioned whether the issue of whether Sylvia could raise a procedural question was properly before the committee, since no advance written notice had been given of her intention to raise it. He wondered if it wouldn't be more appropriate to defer action until the next meeting, when it could be properly noticed up.

Second Vice Chairman Lance Byte, speaking in support of Percy, noted that the question had not yet been referred to the appropriate sections of the firm for their comments, nor had other interested committees been afforded the opportunity to give their views on the matter.

Chairman Phelps said that he would refer it to committee. There was, however, a problem. Since the committee had concurred that it would be out of order for Sylvia to raise her procedural question, how could he determine the appropriate committee to which to refer the question?

Percy said that he was certainly not one to stand on ceremony and that, speaking only for himself, since, he admitted, he had not been authorized to speak for anyone else, he would have no objection if Sylvia whispered the question to the Chairman for the sole purpose of allowing him to make a committee assignment, it being understood that this whispering would not constitute having raised the issue at the meeting.

There being no objections, the committee took a five-minute whisper break.

When the committee reconvened, Chairman Phelps said that the first agenda item was the suggestion from several members of the firm that the method of selecting COBRA members be altered. To refresh the recollection of committee members, since most of them had been on COBRA so long they probably had forgotten how they got there in the first place, the Chairman recognized Fourth Vice Chairman Ellen Jane Ritton, Chair of the Bylaws Subcommittee.

Ellen Jane thanked the Chairman for recognizing her. The Chairman said that Ellen Jane was quite welcome, he was just doing his job. "And very well, too," added Ms. Ritton. The Chairman thanked Ellen Jane, and Ellen Jane said that he was more than welcome.

Ellen Jane then described the method of selection of committee members:

"Partners in the firm were divided initially into groups by judicial district, in accordance with their places of birth. The Nominating Subcommittee was composed of a member from each of seven judicial districts. The seven districts were selected by lot, and the representative from each district was the winner of the bingo game held by that district. The Nominating Subcommittee was charged with making the initial selection of COBRA members, which included the somewhat anomalous job of electing an immediate past chairman and a past immediate past chairman. The Nominating Subcommittee elected themselves to fill all of the COBRA positions, thus creating vacancies in the Nominating Subcommittee, which were filled in the same manner as the original appointments. The bylaws provide that, once elected, committee members move up from fourth vice chairman to chairman, then to immediate past chairman, and then to fourth vice chairman again. The function of the Nominating Subcommittee is currently to fill vacancies on COBRA as they arise due to death or retirement."

Chairman Phelps thanked Ellen Jane, who said not to mention it. He then announced that it had been suggested that the Nominating Subcommittee be given power to select the fourth vice chairman each year. This, it was argued, would make things more democratic and would also provide for some turnover on the committee. There followed a rather lengthy, but inconclusive, debate on the advantages and disadvantages of democracy in the governance of countries, law firms, and bar-related committees.

Sylvia pointed out that, although the proposal would provide some turnover, it would deprive the committee of a measure of continuity by foisting a new member on them every year. The proposal also could lead to scars on the psyches of the person who would be forced off of the committee each year, not to mention the hurt that would be caused to candidates who lost in their bids to become fourth vice chairman. There would be the further problem of when to start this new system. It hardly seemed fair to subject existing members, who had relied on the fact that they would serve for life, to this new rule.

Speaking off the record, Percifal said that he thought the committee would have to come up with some change in the method of selection, since he sensed that opinion around the firm was running rather strongly in favor of the proposal. Asked what he based his statement on, Percy said that he regarded the rash of fires that had broken out in COBRA wastebaskets lately as more than coincidental.

Chairman Phelps said that the problem was not so much that the Nominating Subcommittee would have a chance to appoint somebody to COBRA, but that the person they selected would eventually assume a leadership position.

"What," he suggested, "if we create a new position, fifth vice chairman, and let the Nominating Subcommittee fill that. The bylaws would provide that the other members continue to rotate the way that they currently do. The fifth vice chairman, instead of moving up, will move down to sixth, seventh, and finally eighth vice chairman, at which time he will rotate off of the committee, and the Nominating Subcommittee will select a new fifth vice chairman."

"But, Garrison, do you think that would work?" asked Ellen Jane.

"Of course it would. Nobody reads the bylaws anyway. We just present it as a compromise. They wanted to appoint the fourth vice chairman; we let them have the fifth."

"Brilliant, Gar," said Lance. "And speaking of a fifth, isn't it about time we adjourned?"

"But what about all of those matters of substance," asked Ellen Jane: "the new Model Rules of Professional Conduct, funding for legal services for the poor, individual rights, world peace through law?"

"I move we defer them all," said Percifal. "They all need further study."

"But we've come all the way to Fairbanks, Alaska, and we haven't accomplished anything," said Sylvia sadly.

"Oh, yes we have," objected Chairman Phelps. "We've protected the integrity of our leadership selection process. And that's crucial if we're to have a strong and effective

Bar-Related Activities committee. We can deal with substantive questions any old time, as long as we've got healthy leadership coming up though the ranks. Those problems have been with us for decades; they won't go away. We'll pick them up again at the annual meeting in August."

"Where is the annual meeting this year?" asked Percifal.

"Quito, Ecuador."

Mothers of Invention

What I'm going to say about women lawyers is probably unconstitutional, immoral and generally unwise. But it's the way many of my sex and sexual persuasion view things, I think. So, right or wrong, it may be worth considering. In any case, I didn't get to where I am by keeping my mouth shut, so here goes.

We law firms don't have the foggiest notion what to do about women lawyers. That's my considered opinion, anyway. And here's why—we're men.

Now I recognize that my view may be vulnerable on a couple of grounds. It assumes that men can't understand women. And it fails to recognize that there are some women partners around law firms. I'll grant you both of those. But I don't think either detracts from the fundamental truth of my statement.

Let's get into a bit of history here. Know how many women there were in my law school class? Zero. Know how many there were for twenty-five years or so after that? Zero, plus a couple here and there. With no (or damn few) women lawyers around, it was tough to learn to understand them. When you look at the makeup of law school classes today and see 40% or more women, it's easy to forget what a recent phenomenon that is—twenty years, at best, that we've had women in any numbers in the law schools. So we're not working with a whole lot of history here. And law firms are not exactly famous for their swift adjustments to new conditions.

Even the above assessment of women's presence in law firms is generous. Once women appeared on the law school scene in numbers, they were not exactly absorbed straight into the bloodstream of large law firms.

At first, we firms resisted hiring them at all. In some cases, this was the result of subtle and probably unintentional discrimination. For example, women were passed over because they didn't appear to be aggressive enough (or seemed too aggressive), when the same characteristics were never remarked on for male students. In other cases, the discrimination was more overt: women weren't serious about lawyering, they'd have babies, clients wouldn't want to deal with them.

Jane Hokum-Cohen told me that one partner (at another firm) asked her whether she would be prepared to have an abortion if she were due to have a child in the middle of a big case. Jane aborted the interview, reported the incident, and the firm involved was barred from interviewing at her law school for three years. Most of us large firms dodged a lot of bullets in the form of discrimination law suits that could have been brought by female law students in the seventies, but weren't. Fortunately for us, the statute of limitations has now run.

And when women were hired, we often pigeonholed them into areas of the law that were thought appropriate for women—estate planning, real estate (house deals), divorce, tax, but not litigation or corporate. We relegated our first woman lawyer, Felicia Grundy, to house deals. She lasted two years before resigning. Not coincidentally, her resignation came the day after closing a complicated million-and-a-half-dollar house deal for one of my biggest clients, who told her to "please thank Mr. Fairweather for me, Sweetie Pie."

It wasn't until fifteen years ago that our firm had a woman in either our corporate or litigation departments. And when women finally did make it into the mainstream, they had to work their way up the ladder, first to partner and then to a place in the management of the firm. That takes time.

While all of this was happening, who was left to deal with women's issues? Men. And in dealing (or not dealing) with these issues, we men faced many obstacles.

First, as I said earlier, was understanding women. I'll admit, I used to think that was a bogus issue. But I no longer do. Maggie's convinced me otherwise. (Indeed, any insights found in this chapter ought to be credited to her. I was about as poor at understanding women as anyone I know.) As she and I have talked, I think I've come to better understand women and what they face. But I've still got a long way to go.

Part of the problem, I think, is that we male partners didn't *want* to understand women. Trying to understand them was as much a pain as trying to understand our wives (which I, for one, flunked cold). We had other, more important things to do, like practice law. And besides, it wasn't necessary to understand them. We men knew how to practice law. Hell, we'd been practicing it without women all these years just fine, hadn't we? If women wanted to practice, they'd just have to adjust to the way it had always been done, play the game the same way we did.

In this view, we were supported by a seemingly unlikely source—women partners who had succeeded in our firm. If you don't believe me, ask my partners Ruth Tender and Jane Hokum-Cohen. If they're candid, I think they'll admit that they were very tough on the women who followed them. Ruth and Jane had made it, hadn't they? Why couldn't others do the same? After all, if you really wanted to succeed at the firm, you had to be willing to make some sacrifices. What these successful women partners were really saying is, if they admitted that some adjustments, however reasonable, were necessary for women, it might diminish the respect in which they were held by the firm. And they were probably right.

How did we break out of this circle? Well, I don't think we have, yet. But we're making some progress, for four reasons. First, there's the law. Discrimination against women is illegal. As lawyers, that ought to mean something to us. Second, there have been some courageous women lawyers who have spoken out. Third, men have changed. Not so much old codgers like me, but the new generation of men, my younger partners who will never know how it is to make decisions about women without women to listen to and argue with. Many of them have wives who are battling the same battles as the women at our firm. Needless to say, that makes those fellas a bit more sympathetic to the problems of our women lawyers than men of my generation. And the fourth reason, and most powerful of all, is necessity, the mother of invention.

Fact is that many of the best lawyers floating around this country today happen to be of the female persuasion. And if we need the best legal talent available to do our work, much of that talent is going to be women. If we have to find a way to adjust to keep that talent around, we'll find it. Even men respond to necessity.

But even more important, some of the upper echelons of corporate America are beginning to be inhabited by women. So it just might be in our law firm's interest to have some women at the top of our structure, for business reasons. Bingo. Ruth is a very capable lawyer. But she's not the youngest member of our Executive Committee through pure chance.

Now that leaves us with the *real* problems. Our firm is not a factory, not yet, thank goodness. We can't just pull somebody out of the line and plop down someone new with no effect on the work. Not everything can be done on a 9 to 5 schedule. Emergencies do arise. Needs vary from department to department.

So how do we handle things? Job sharing? Part-time work? What part? Leaves of absence? For how long? Extending the length of the partnership track? By how much? Is every option available to everyone, or does it vary by department, or by individual? Where are the glass ceilings and how do you raise them? What's sexual harassment, and how do you prevent it?

These are tough questions. Darn tough. And I don't think we've come close to answering them. Frankly, I'm still not quite sure that we men have developed enough will, become convinced enough of the seriousness of the problems, to tackle the tougher questions.

Sometimes I think I liked things a whole lot better when the answers were simple, when the only flack I caught was for being a male chauvinist pig. Why? For such serious offenses as asking Bertha to bring coffee into my office several times a day. Now nobody seems to pay any attention to us male chauvinist pigs anymore. Oink.

Ugly as SIN

As I said, not so long ago women were a rather scarce commodity in our firm. As they became less scarce, we had to try to figure out what the hell we were going to do with them. To give you some idea of how our firm struggled with the "woman problem" (as we used to call it), I've salvaged the minutes of a 1979 meeting of a subcommittee of our Executive Committee.

"What are we going to call ourselves?" asked Oscar Winters.

"I'm going to call myself Bob," answered Robert Mentor.

"No, I mean this subcommittee. We're supposed to deal with the woman problem, but I don't like the ring of 'Woman Problem Subcommittee.' "

"We could call it the 'Subcommittee on Sexual Equality,'" suggested Stephen Falderall.

"Sounds very 1960ish. Sheldon Horvitz would love it," commented Mentor.

"I'm not sure *I* like it," said Nails Nuttree. "What does 'equality' mean, anyway? We may be opening a whole can of worms."

"Well, I certainly don't want to do that. I'm extremely anti-worm," announced Oscar.

"Why do we have to name the subcommittee anything?" asked Mentor.

"I'm pretty sure the firm handbook requires it. Anyway, it's traditional, and I don't think we should just thumb our noses at tradition because of some women," said Oscar.

"Okay, then why don't we call it something innocuous, like the 'Subcommittee on Sex in the Law Firm,' " suggested Stephen.

"No, nothing with 'sex' in it. And your suggestion doesn't form an acronym, anyway," complained Oscar.

"Fine, then how about 'Subcommittee on Institutional Non-discrimination,' SIN," suggested Stephen, which suggestion was adopted unanimously by the subcommittee.

"Exactly what do we consider to be the 'woman problem'?" asked Stephen.

"Well, we are getting more and more women lawyers around the firm," said Oscar.

"Yes?"

"And they're, well, different," continued Oscar.

"I've noticed that myself," commented Nails.

"I mean, how can we send them out to clients? What would our clients think?" asked Oscar.

"Confidentially, I see that as something of a problem myself," said Robert. "I mean clients are guys. And guys talk about different things than girls."

"Such as what?" asked Stephen.

"Such as sports, for instance."

"What makes you think women can't talk about sports?" asked Robert. "My wife knows more about the Bears than I do. And Stanley's secretary, Bertha, can tell you the lifetime batting average of Harry Chitti."

"Who the hell is Harry Chitti?"

"See what I mean. Harry Chitti was one of a long string of inept Cub catchers. A walk when old Harry was catching was as good as a triple for the opposition. The runner would go on the first pitch, Harry would play the ball off of the wall behind the plate and then he'd toss it into center field."

"Well, even if some girls can talk about sports, there are other things guys talk about that would not be appropriate for girls."

"For example?"

"Girls."

"Well, maybe guys would just have to not talk about 'girls,' as you call them, in front of women," said Stephen.

"It's not just talking about girls," explained Oscar. "Clients just aren't used to seeing girl lawyers. They wouldn't want anything important to be handled by them."

"Then we'll just have to show them that the women we've hired are every bit as good as the male lawyers we have," said Stephen.

"But there are some very practical problems," said Nails. "In my experience, women tend to have babies."

"You *are* a man-of-the-world," said Stephen.

"And when they do, they may disappear, right in the middle of a trial. Men don't do that, in my experience."

"Well, maybe we could hire around that problem," suggested Oscar.

"What do you mean?" asked Bob.

"Well, first of all, we could stay away from the married ones."

"It's against the law to ask if they're married," said Stephen.

"I'm too clever to fall into that trap. You don't have to ask, just look for the ring."

"You're clever alright, Oscar, but it's still illegal."

"Well, how about just hiring ugly ones, then? Ugliness isn't a protected class yet, is it?"

"No, as long as you're going to hire only ugly men, also."

"This is going to be a hell of a pleasant place to work," said Nails. "Everyone walking the halls is going to be ugly as sin."

"Confidentially, I'm not that comfortable with the number of women we've been hiring," said Bob. "I'm afraid we'll get to be known around law schools as a women's firm. And then we won't be able to hire the guys we want."

"Yes, and besides, a lot of these women have husbands who have very good jobs," added Oscar. "I spoke to one whose husband was a doctor, for heaven's sake. They don't really need these positions, and they're taking them away from guys who do."

"Now, I'm not prejudiced myself," said Nails, "but I do have to say that I don't think women are tough enough to be litigators. I mean, not many of them have played football or served in the marines. If I found one who did, I'd be the first to hire her."

"I can hardly believe what I'm hearing," said Stephen. "I'd have expected it ten or twenty years ago, but not today. You're trotting out all of the old stereotypes that I thought we'd left behind. And *we're* the committee that's supposed to be dealing with the future of women at the firm. I think we need a woman on this committee."

"Impossible," said Oscar. "This is a subcommittee of the Executive Committee and we don't have any women on the Executive Committee."

"Well, maybe it shouldn't be a subcommittee of the Executive Committee then," suggested Stephen.

"But it is," insisted Oscar. "Just look around: we're all members of the EC. And if we were to put a woman on this committee, we couldn't have the sort of frank discussion that we're having now with just us guys."

"Well, this frank discussion isn't getting us anywhere. And it's a little too frank for me," said Stephen.

"I suppose we could invite one of our woman lawyers, as a guest, to our next meeting," said Nails. "Of course, she wouldn't have a vote. And there might be a few times that we'd want her to excuse herself, go to the ladies room you know, so that we could talk man-to-man."

"Well, who would we invite as a guest?" asked Bob.

"Ruth Tender is the most senior," observed Oscar. "So I suppose it should be her."

"No, if we have to invite somebody, how about that Jane Hokum-Cohen? I hear she was a damn good field hockey player. And she's vavavaVOOM, if you know what I mean," said Nails.

"Nails, Jane's married and so are you," reminded Oscar.

"Yes, but I'm not blind."

[STANLEY'S NOTE: Jane's guest appearance at the next SIN meeting was a turning point in the history of women at our firm. Not only did she refuse to excuse herself to go to the ladies room (she said she didn't have to go), but she insisted on reporting on the meeting to all associates. Shortly thereafter, the original SIN was dissolved.]

Overperfection

Practice may make perfect, but we lawyers are in danger of overperfection. Serious danger, I'm afraid. In the days of carbon paper . . . Is there carbon paper anymore? Has the entire carbon paper industry disappeared? Was there really a time when we practiced law without xerox . . . I mean photocopy machines?

I know that I can't talk about xerox machines or xeroxing, or I'll get a letter from the legal department of Xerox Corporation telling me not to do that. That's how lawyers keep busy: combing books and periodicals to make sure that nobody is talking about their corporation or product in a way that could endanger their trademark or trade name or something.

I am reminded of Groucho Marx's wonderful correspondence with the legal department of Warner Brothers, which appears in *The Groucho Letters*. In the early 1940s, that legal department wrote a letter attempting to dissuade Marx from using the title *A Night in Casablanca* because of its similarity to *Casablanca*, made five years earlier.

In several hilarious letters, Groucho suggests, among other things, "that the average movie fan could learn in time to distinguish between Ingrid Bergman and Harpo," and questions whether Warner Brothers has the right to use the word "Brothers," since "Professionally, we were brothers even before you were . . . and even before us there had been other brothers—the Smith Brothers; the Brothers Karamazov; Dan Brothers, an outfielder with Detroit; and 'Brother, Can You Spare a Dime?' " These letters apparently drove the Warner Brothers legal department bonkers, and the matter was dropped.

Where were we? Oh yes: practicing law before the advent of the photocopy machine. Production was a real problem then. Let's say you wanted ten copies of something. You typed an original and then used nine sheets of carbon paper, each followed by a sheet of paper behind the original. Remember, we're talking about real, mechanical typewriters here. These were the stone ages, before we even had electric typewriters.

If you wanted more copies than you could produce through carbon paper, you could mimeograph. That involved typing your document onto a stencil, fastening the stencil to a round drum and rotating the drum while feeding paper through so that the ink would be transferred from the stencil to the paper. This could well be the messiest process ever invented by man to do anything. I may still have traces of ink on my left hand from my stint as a mimeograph boy in high school.

But what does all of this have to do with perfection? Well, let's suppose Bertha has just typed an original and nine copies of a contract I'd written. She's an excellent typist and doesn't make many mistakes. When she did make a mistake, though, she'd have to take the sheet out of the typewriter, erase (we didn't even have whiteout) the original and each of the copies, reinsert the page and try to line it up exactly, then make the correction. Bertha doesn't swear, but she sure can make "gracious" sound like a pretty mean word, I'll tell you.

So now Bertha has finished typing the document and has brought it in for me to review. I've heard a few "gracious"es from outside my office. I look it over: looks pretty good. Sure, there are some possible changes that occur to me, but I weigh pretty carefully whether those changes are important enough to ask Bertha to make them ten times over. I'd sooner incur the wrath of God than the look I'd get from my beloved secretary (and believe me, Bertha knows important from unimportant).

Fast forward to today. I get the same document back. There's only one copy, not ten. During its production I've heard no "gracious"es, since the few mistakes Bertha may make are word processed away in no time. I look it over. Looks pretty good. Some changes occur to me. I make them. It comes back again. I make more changes. Back again. I switch some things back to the way I had them originally. (I'm like the fellow who only made one mistake in his life: the time he thought he'd done something wrong, when really it was right.)

I don't worry about Bertha's reaction to my changes. It only takes her a minute to revise. And if she's too busy, I can always send it up to the word-processing pool to revise. I don't worry about getting it in the mail for the 5 o'clock pickup: nobody uses the mail for anything important, anyway. It's all express delivery services or fax machines. (No wonder our regular mail is so dull.) We complain about increases of pennies in postage, but the fact is, we've accepted the need to pay ten bucks or more for what used to be a first-class letter.

Have I produced a better document through all of my revisions? Perhaps, marginally. But was it worth bettering? Lawyers never ask that question. We're all trained to do everything to perfection. In law school, we second-guess Supreme Court justices. We strive for the top of the class and the law reviews, and look down on those who don't make it. In large firms we're coached to do things over and over again until they're perfect. Too often, if we had bothered to ask the question of whether something was worth bettering, the candid answer would have been, "to me, yes—I'm paid by the hour; to my client, no—he's paying the bill."

Well, I think we'd better start asking that question pretty soon. Of course, I'm not talking here about changes that are important to the substance of a document. That's not overperfection, that's professionalism. But we'd better start appreciating the difference between a bell or a whistle and an engine. We'd better start producing documents whose style is good enough, not perfect; prose, not poetry. Because our penchant for stylistic perfection is making us plain unaffordable to too many clients. And even the clients who can afford us don't always want a Mercedes Benz. Sometimes a Volkswagen will do. If we don't build one for them, they'll find somebody who will.

Maybe we should bring back carbon paper.

Don't Blindly Copy Unless You See Why

Although carbon paper has gone the way of the brontysaurus, "cc"s have not. Each year, our firm publishes a newly-revised edition of *Style and Grace in FWS Documents*, which prescribes guidelines for all FWS communications, internal and external.

Bound in genuine cowhide, most FWS secretaries agree that it is a good value at the $80 price they are required to pay for it. The 1993 edition is over 700 pages long, and each copy is personally autographed by Howard Punctillio, Chair of the Committee on Firm Forms (COFF) and editor of the book. Here is a section from the latest edition.

Chapter LXXIV
Section 9
Subsection K:
Copies of Letters

There are thousands of ways to send copies of letters. Your boss will know most of these tricks, but it may help you to appreciate just how clever he or she is being by understanding some of the subtleties. Here are a few:

(1) One way to send a letter to two people is to write and actually address the letter to both people. This generally will be done when the two people are of roughly equal stature and are at two different places of work. Thus, an attorney preparing a contract involving two other parties

might send the contract with a cover letter addressed to counsel for each of the other two parties.

NOTE: In this situation you need only concern yourself with which attorney's name appears on the left-hand side of the letter (generally the more important), and which gets the original (generally the one on the left, unless you are to produce two originals or unless your boss wants to take both of them down a peg by sending them both copies, or wants to balance the situation by sending the one on the left a copy while consoling the poor person who wound up on the right by sending him or her the original).

(2) Another possibility is to send the same letter to two people, addressing each letter only to the individual who is to receive it. This is used frequently where the likelihood of the two recipients finding out that they each received the same letter is remote. Thus, if your boss has just had an extensive research job done on a question that has application to two or more clients, identical but separate letters may be sent setting forth the results of the research. Such a technique may permit billing both clients for the work or, at least, showing the client who is not billed how on top of recent developments your boss is. In this case, be sure you do a global change of the names between the two letters. It weakens the personal touch a bit if you start the letter to Fred out with "Dear Sally."

(3) A third method is to address the letter to one person and send a copy to another, indicating the copy with a "cc:" at the bottom ("cc:" stands for "carbon copy" and is a throwback to the days when carbon paper was used. It should now be changed to "xc," but inertia has probably prevented this to date). This technique may be used:
    (a) Where the addressee is the primary recipient and the person who receives the "cc" is merely being kept appraised either
        (i) because of a need to know, or

(ii) because he or she is paying the bills and should see how much work is going into the job, or

(b) to indicate to the primary addressee that he or she better beware because somebody else is reviewing the transaction, or

(c) because the person receiving the "cc" has at least as great a need to know as the primary addressee, but is less significant.

NOTE: Of course, more than one person may receive a "cc," in which case those receiving a "cc" may be listed in order of importance or, where there is doubt as to the relative importance of the "cc" recipients, alphabetically.

(4) Next, there is the use of the "bcc" or "blind carbon copy," where the primary addressee is unaware that the "bcc" is receiving a copy, which may be employed

(a) to give the "bcc" a cheap thrill, akin to participation in illicit sex (a "bcc" being the closest most lawyers ever come to that);

(b) to show off for the client where your boss has written a real zinger of a letter to the other side and wants the client to get a load of it, even though that is really not necessary;

(c) where your boss is sending a copy to another lawyer in the firm and does not want the client to be aware that it is being charged for both lawyers' time on the letter (of course, a lawyer at a firm who receives a "bcc" should be on guard, since it generally means that the person sending the letter is scheming to take charge of the client); and,

(d) to protect the letter writer's ass by allowing him or her, when the shit hits the fan because of the contents of the letter, to point to the fact that one or more additional people were aware of what was going on and failed to act.

NOTE: Of course, there may be "bcc"s with or without "cc"s and some or all of the "cc"s may be made aware of the "bcc"s and, in the case of multiple "bcc"s, some "bcc"s may be aware of other "bcc"s and others not—the possibilities for intrigue are nearly endless.

(5) There is also the stilted method of sending a copy by utilizing language in the body of the letter, such as "By copy of this letter I am sending the agreement to Mr. Nasaltwitch for his review and comment." This generally will be used by lawyers over sixty years of age, or by those who are attempting to compensate for their failure to attend an effete Eastern law school by using language every bit as pretentious as that used by Yale graduates.

(6) Both "cc"s and "bcc"s may be sent with enclosures, indicated as "w/encl.," or without. A person who receives a "cc" or "bcc" without an enclosure presumably need only know that the document enclosed has been sent, but needn't know beans about the contents of the enclosure; thus, "w/out encl." is generally reserved for real higher-ups, like top corporate executives and law partners, who probably wouldn't understand the enclosure if they received it, anyway. Occasionally, "w/out encl." is used to save on the photocopying bill.

(6.5) Of course, there are many possibilities for the creative use of the "cc" and the "bcc," with or without enclosures. For example, the "cc w/encl." may be used without sending the enclosure. This will permit the sender of the letter another two or three days to produce the enclosure, and can cut two or three days off the time that an opponent can review the document prior to a meeting or hearing.

(7) Another possibility is to send somebody a "cc" without sending the actual letter, of which the "cc" is

supposedly a copy, to the addressee. This may be done as a practical joke, as, for example, where the supposed original letter is outrageously rude or where it contains information that the recipient of the "cc" would not want the addressee of the letter to receive. Much the same effect may be achieved by indicating a "cc" on the original letter, but not actually sending the "cc." This is very clever, so if your boss does it and you value your job—laugh. Uproariously.

Now I'm sure that the section of the manual I've quoted does not exhaust all of the possibilities for sending copies. But it exhausts enough of them. At least it exhausts me.

De-honing Legal Minds

Certain things you can count on hearing every year, and one of them is, "They don't have any idea how to practice law." The "they," of course, is our new associates, the best and the brightest from the top law schools around the country. And the people saying it are my partners, all of whom ought to find this state of affairs completely unremarkable, as they've been complaining about it at least since they became partners (and the precocious ones, since they were second-year associates).

I've taken to responding to these comments with something like, "No, and they can't perform open heart surgery, either." This generally brings my partners up short, and I am greeted with either a quizzical look or a "what?" I go on to explain that law school sets out to teach students neither how to practice law nor how to perform open heart surgery—and it succeeds quite brilliantly at both. In fact, as a rule, the more prestigious the law school, the less it prepares its students to practice. This is because those elite schools bristle at the notion that they are "trade schools," and concentrate instead on honing the finest legal minds in a way that equips them best to follow in the footsteps of those who are doing the honing. So we law firms are left to de-hone, re-hone and post-hone those fine legal minds so that they become a modicum of use to our clients in helping to solve their real-life problems. And when we're unsuccessful, some of our brightest associates leave the firm and return to law school to teach our next generation of lawyers.

Let's leave aside the question of whether law schools should be producing practicing lawyers. One can argue both sides of that question. Whichever side you choose, the fact is that the situation is unlikely to change materially. I'll concede that with their clinical programs and all, law schools are doing a marginally better job preparing students for practice than they were back when I was in school. But, even if they wanted to, how could law schools prepare their students for practice when they are staffed almost entirely by professors who have little, if any, experience practicing themselves (the more prestigious the school, the less the faculty knows about practicing at any level below the Supreme Court).

Have you ever thought of the implications of this for the way we go about choosing our future lawyers? Because we don't have much confidence in our ability to select the students who possess the personal qualities to succeed in the practice, we focus on their grades. As a result, we wind up choosing one law student over another because some constitutional law professor who hasn't practiced law a day in his life thought he wrote a slightly better exam than the person sitting next to him. Good, independent judgment, eh?

The result of law schools' approach to teaching is that each year we law firms harvest a brilliant crop of new associates who are trained to think like lawyers, but not to act like them. Take, for example, Rudy Flauntem, whose brief career with us came to a screeching halt fifteen years ago when he announced to the executive vice president of one of my clients that his proposed solution to a problem was "simple-minded and lacked even a rudimentary appreciation for the complexity of the Internal Revenue Code provision involved." That arrogance may fly in a law school classroom—or in a Supreme Court dissenting opinion—but not in real life. (Rudy has found his niche. He now teaches conflicts of law at a national law school and has been mentioned prominently as a candidate for appointment to the Seventh Circuit.) This gap between thinking and acting like a lawyer provides the grist that keeps six or eight of our firm committees' mills grinding. And yet, because market forces have conspired to require us to pay these new lawyers enormous salaries, we are constrained to bill them out to our clients at $120 an hour. That may have worked in the blissful, Big-Rock-Candy-Mountain days when clients were foolish enough to pay us at whatever hourly rate we decided to bill for our new associates. But it won't work anymore. That same $120 will buy an hour of the time of a plumber, an electrician or a carpenter, each of whom is trained to do the work that he is doing. Most clients would rather have the plumber, electrician or carpenter. And I can't say that I blame them.

So what to do about all of this? Given my druthers, I'd opt for the English and Canadian approach. They recognize that the person coming out of law school is not ready to practice. So before they are authorized to practice ("called to the Bar" as they put it—would that more of *our* young lawyers felt "called" to the Bar), law graduates must spend time apprenticing as article clerks (rhymes with "sparks"). During this apprenticeship period, it's the firms' obligation to train them and to pay them a salary commensurate with somebody who is being trained. I've never quite understood how our medical profession managed to accomplish this with their interns and residents and we in the legal profession missed the boat completely.

For whatever reason, though, I suppose that boat left the dock long ago. Maybe some firms will have the guts (or, what's perhaps more likely, be forced by economic necessity) to cut back the salaries of young associates. Frankly, I think many of our new associates might welcome that. They know they're not worth what we're paying them. (I've had several of our new associates say to me over the years, "I can't believe this; I'm making more money than my father has *ever* made in his life.") And being paid more than you know you're worth adds a lot of additional stress to what's already a plenty stressful situation.

Or perhaps we'll invent a less radical form of articling. How about this for a message to new associates?

'Welcome to Fairweather, Winters & Sommers. We're very impressed with your law school accomplishments but, frankly, we don't think that experience has taught you much about how to practice law. We think you learn how to practice best through working with and watching the best lawyers in action. So, for the first two months of your tenure with us, we are going to assign you to two partners at our firm. Your job will be to follow them around, watch what they do and how they do it, and learn as much as you can from that experience. If you can help them out on a project that they're working on, fine. Maybe you'll bill a few hours. But we're not expecting that.

'Since you're not going to be contributing to the firm's work during those two months, we're going to reduce your first year's salary by one-sixth. So you can have a steady stream of income, though, we'll spread your ten months' salary equally over the year. We expect to benefit from the experience you'll be getting during those first two months, too, over time. So, if you remain with our firm for three years, we'll pay you an extra bonus equal to the two months salary that you didn't receive in your first year.'

Listen to me. There I go, suggesting new (and perhaps hare-brained) ideas. That wasn't the purpose of writing this book. But, truth is, I can't help myself. When you've been thinking constantly all these years about what might make your firm a better place, you don't just turn off the spigot without an occasional drip.

Less Than Super-vision

The firm committee charged with associate training is CARE (the Committee on Associate Retention and Evaluation). Training was the topic of discussion at a recent meeting of CARE, the minutes of which appear below.

Committee Chair Stephen Falderall called the meeting to order at 12:15. And again at 12:25, and 12:30. At 12:40, he threatened to withhold dessert unless the meeting quieted down promptly, which it did.

"I apologize, but I have to leave at 12:45," said Franklin Goodtime.

"But that's only five minutes from now," said Falderall.

"Four by my watch," corrected Goodtime.

"Then why did you bother coming?" asked the Chair.

"It was no bother," assured Frank. "And the meeting was called for noon, so I thought I'd have forty-five minutes."

"You know very well that our meetings never start when they're called," said Harold Ratchet.

"That's not my fault," said Frank.

"We're not talking about fault, we're talking about why you came to the meeting. And it looks to me like you came just for lunch," said Ellen Jane Ritton.

"Why, that's outrageous! Take that back right now!" demanded Frank. "I came because I'm dedicated to the committee's work."

"I will *not* take it back, because it's true."

"I'm not going to have us getting into this kind of character assassination, Ellen Jane, even if it is true. I want to get on with our agenda, which is devoted to training," said the Chair.

"Thanks, Steve. Now I *do* have to take off. Mind if I grab one of these apple tarts for the road; they look scrumptious," said Frank, leaving.

"I rest my case," said Ellen Jane.

"Can we please get to training?" pleaded the Chair.

"I think our training is going great guns," opined Lancelot Byte. "My presentation entitled, 'The Two Things Nobody Can Avoid Rolled Into One: Death Taxes' was extremely well received last month."

"How many people attended?" asked Hector Morgan.

"Oh, quite a few," said Lance.

"What's quite a few?"

"It's hard to say exactly, but I'd estimate it at around four."

"Does that include you, Lance?" asked Harold.

"Of course it includes me; I attended."

"And were the other three from your department?" asked the Chair.

"Two of them were."

"Well, that sort of defeats the purpose of the program, which is to familiarize lawyers in other departments with what you're doing, so that they can cross-sell to their clients. Who was the third?" asked the Chair.

"Florence."

"Your wife came?"

"She loves to hear me speak. And besides, she held up some cue cards to remind me of the next topic as we went along."

"I don't know why we knock ourselves out doing these CLE programs if nobody attends," said Hector.

"Well, with all due respect to Lance, I'm not sure that

death taxes is the sexiest topic for young lawyers at the firm," said the Chair.

"That may be so," said Harold, "but even in our more glamorous areas we don't exactly seem to be turning people away at the door for these things. In fact, I had my secretary pull together the attendance figures for the last nine CLE programs we've run, and we seem to hit double digits only when we offer dinner with the program."

"Maybe we should make more use of our high-tech capabilities. We bought all of that video equipment, but we hardly ever use it," said the Chair.

"I hear that Manny Candoo tried to use it in his securities law session, but he grabbed the wrong tape, and the group had to watch his daughter's wedding reception," said Hector.

"I don't think it's a matter of high tech versus low tech," said Harold. "These substantive law programs are too much like law school. Young associates are sick of them. I think we need more skills training; that's what they really want."

"Well, Nails did that deposition skills class. How did that go?" asked Ellen Jane.

"Miserably. Three associates left the firm within a week after the program," said Hector.

"What went wrong?" asked Ellen Jane.

"Everything. Nails sat in on all of the depositions, and every time anyone did something Nails thought he could have been done better, he honked a horn to stop the deposition and corrected the error."

"He didn't."

"Oh yes he did," said Hector. "I was walking by the conference room with one of my clients and he wanted to know whether there were geese in there."

"Are we sure that the associates left for that reason, though? Maybe it was just coincidental," asked Ellen Jane.

"Pretty sure," answered Hector. "On their last day in the office, all three of them dressed like Harpo and honked their way out of the reception area at five."

"That's terrible," said Ellen Jane. "But I think we're barking up the wrong tree, anyway, in these CLE programs—substantive or skills. I don't think that's what associates are after."

"What do they want, then?" asked the Chair.

"They want hands-on, on-the-job training. They want supervision and feedback from the partners they work with. That's what they want."

"Well, we've tried to convince our partners to do that every way I can think of, but it hasn't worked," said the Chair.

"What have we tried? That must have been before my time," asked Ellen Jane.

"First we tried a memo circulated by me on the importance of partners providing supervision and feedback."

"And what happened?"

"Everybody agreed it was important, and nobody did anything about it. Then we hired somebody to come in and teach our partners how to provide good supervision and feedback."

"That sounds like a good idea. What happened? Did they give any more feedback?"

"Yes, they told our consultant that they didn't like what he was teaching them and suggested something to him."

"What did they suggest?"

"That he try another field, like sky diving. And then the next thing the firm tried was adopting a policy that supervision would be taken into consideration in determining partners' compensation."

"Well, that ought to have provided a strong incentive for partners to improve their supervision efforts."

"It might have, but Stanley makes all of our final compensation decisions and he has a policy of never telling anybody why. So nobody believed that supervision would help their compensation. And nothing else we've tried has worked, either."

"I've got an idea that might work," said Ellen Jane.

"Well, out with it, let's hear it," demanded the Chair.

"We've got to figure out a way to punish partners for failing to give supervision. Threatening to cut their percentage hasn't worked, but maybe we can make failure to give supervision carry with it a burden so onerous that nobody would be willing to accept it."

"Sounds good, but what do you have in mind?"

"How about service on this committee. I can't think of a more thankless task than that."

"Good idea, Ellen Jane. I'll get a memo out on it right away."

[STANLEY'S NOTE: Ellen Jane's idea, like everything else the committee had tried, was unsuccessful in getting partners to provide supervision and feedback. Within three months, membership on CARE had swelled to seventy-six, so I felt obliged to tell the committee to back off on its threat.]

Safari, So Goody

One of the best vacations I ever took was a photo safari to Africa—Kenya and Tanzania. After a trip like that, it's tough to visit zoos (except, of course, with your grandchild). On that trip I developed a sense of awe for the animals I saw, their beauty and grace of movement, their size and coloration, their freedom. Nobody can return from such a trip unmoved. Of course, besides beauty and grace, there's drama and death too. The fleet, the strong and the wily survive; others do not.

I thought a lot about the firm while I was on that safari. I know I shouldn't be thinking about the firm on vacation, but I always do. Anyway, on this trip it was unavoidable. Everywhere I looked, I saw my partners. At first, I began to identify particular species of animals with different areas of our practice. But I quickly realized that that approach was far too simplistic. Why, among our litigators alone we have a giraffe, Percifal Snikkety, who travels quite above the fray; a jaguar, Harvey Holdem, who darts in quickly for the kill; and Nails Nuttree, our bull elephant, who simply tramples anything in his path. By the time I returned, I think I'd spotted every one of my partners, and had photos of most of them.

And my identification of the firm with the wilds did not stop when the safari ended. Listening to my partners after I returned, I was struck by how many of them were treating life at our firm as if it were life in the wild. As we reviewed our associates' performances we would conclude that some of them would have to be "let go" . . . don't you love how we describe chopping somebody's head off as "letting them go." In the animal kingdom, if they could talk, they'd probably call it "setting them free." Come to think of it, I'll bet that many of those we fire, in retrospect, see it as having been set free . . .

Anyway, as we let associates go, one after another of my partners talked about how the associates just didn't have it and hadn't made it. In discussing the reasons why the promising attorneys we'd just recently recruited so enthusiastically from top schools around the country had not worked out, some of my partners acknowledged that perhaps supervision of work was sometimes spotty, or evaluations of work were not always candid or constructive, or senior lawyers did not always take the time to provide the mentoring that young associates needed. But the bottom line assessment was always the same—the associate simply couldn't hack it. "The law business is a tough business today; only the fittest survive," they concluded.

I admit that law is a tough business. I'll even concede that only the fittest survive. To some extent we made sure of that when we over-hired in the boom years of the 80s, so that we needed to fell more associates before they reached the watering hole known as partnership. But law firms still are not (or, at least, should not be) jungles. Unlike jaguars and bull elephants, law firms have considerable control over their environment. Indeed, to a large extent, we create it.

So, not being the shy, retiring type, I spoke out at the meeting. I asked my partners to imagine a firm that rents space on the fiftieth floor of an office building. Though the building has elevators, the firm requires its lawyers to walk up and down the stairs to and from work. For security reasons, the firm purchases two ferocious doberman pinschers, which it does not feed and houses in the reception area. Lawyers coming and leaving must make their way past these killers. To save money, the firm runs the air conditioners only two hours per day during the summer and hires only four secretaries to produce work for fifty lawyers. Finally, because of the scarcity of secretarial services, the firm requires that lawyers send out to clients first drafts of the documents they produce.

Not surprisingly, lawyers leave the firm in droves. The Executive Committee, assessing the reasons for these departures, concludes that the lawyers who left just couldn't hack it. "Law is a tough business," they say; "only the fittest survive."

Several of my partners thought I'd come up with an absurd hypothetical. No law firm in its right mind would allow such obstacles to a lawyer's performance to exist, when they were so clearly within the firm's control.

But how much more sense does it make, I asked, for a firm to spend hundreds of thousands of dollars hiring and training bright lawyers, and then allow them to starve to death, craving morsels of supervision, evaluation and mentoring? Or hamstring lawyers with rules, regulations and procedures that have the effect of caging them? All of these elements are within our control, as well.

Of course, supervision requires greater effort than turning on the air conditioning all day or not allowing dobermans to roam the reception area. These activities take more than money; they take time and effort on the part of lawyers. But I've always thought that the effort pays off handsomely in the long run—in increased productivity, in retention of associates and in greater recruitment success.

Law is indeed a tough business. And only the fittest do survive (with the exception of the occasional brother or niece). But those of us who run law firms can make them far more hospitable jungles—jungles in which more of our young lawyers will succeed. All we need to do is remove a few of the unnecessary obstacles we create and to guide our lawyers a bit more through the inevitable areas of undergrowth before we allow them to roam more freely on the legal plains—and then tame a few of our wildest partners.

The Dearly Departed

Inevitably, we do hire some attorneys who are not fit enough to survive. Worse, some of the fittest choose to leave us. Faced with the need to manage the problem of associates leaving the firm in droves, our Executive Committee circulated this memo recently.

To: All Partners
From: Executive Committee
Subject: Dealing with Associates Leaving the Firm

    The first step in dealing with associates leaving the firm is to admit, at least among ourselves, that associates do leave large law firms. Since four have left ours in the last week and a half, this should be doable.

    Next, we must recognize that our job is merely to explain these leavings in a manner that will permit the remaining associates to differentiate between our firm and the Titanic. The proper way of doing this will vary depending upon the situation surrounding the associate's leaving, the job to which the associate went and the person to whom the leaving is being explained.

    Take first the situation surrounding the associate's leaving. In the case of any associate who is not obviously a star (a star being one who pleased an important partner on his or her most recent assignment) and who is not leaving for an EER, as defined below, we should create the impression that the associate has been told that he or she is not making it. Since this generally will not be true and since this is a firm with integrity, we should take care not to lie openly—or at least not to put it in writing. The desired effect normally can be achieved by an appropriate look, a refusal to comment on other associates' questions as to whether the leaving associate has been asked to leave, and ambiguous statements such as "I am sure that X will be happier elsewhere" or "X will make a fine lawyer—at another firm."

Creating this impression will result in a favorable reaction in associates still at the firm, akin to that experienced by an Army private whose best buddy has just been shrapneled. Since each associate knows, deep down, that a certain number of his *confrères* inevitably will get axed, there is a natural feeling of relief when somebody else gets the blade. Associates may long to get out of here, but they want to do it of their own accord.

Next, let's deal with the case of the star associate who leaves for other than an EER. (An EER, of course, is an easily explicable reason. Such reasons include leaving to teach, to practice poverty law, to assume a lucrative position with the associate's father-in-law's corporation, to became ambassador to Great Britain or to perform magic tricks at birthday parties and bar mitzvahs. All of these provide opportunities not easily matchable by the firm and, therefore, leaving for such a reason does not reflect ill upon the firm. Hence, when an associate leaves for an EER, the firm can risk telling other associates the truth about the leaving.)

But let's assume that the star leaves for a non-EER, say to join a small law firm. There are several acceptable choices for explanations, including (a) Joe was really not cut out for the pressure of the big leagues and he'll be happier with a small firm, (b) Sarah told me that the altitude in our lofty offices was making her vomit thrice daily, so naturally she was reluctantly forced to make the change for health reasons, or (c) Rasputin always wanted a small firm. He thought that when he interviewed us and spoke to seven persons, he had spoken to every lawyer in the firm. When he discovered his mistake, it was inevitable that he would leave.

The far more difficult situation is presented when a star leaves to join another big firm. If the new firm has a strong department not present at our firm, it is possible to explain the leaving in terms of a desire by the associate to practice in this new area. Otherwise, one is left to choose among being philosophical, whimsical or vicious.

The philosophical approach, ideally, should start out with a foreign phrase. "C'est la vie" is appropriate, but hackneyed almost to the point of not being foreign anymore. "Así es la vida" is not bad, but Spanish may not be erudite enough for some. My own favorite is "ein Pferd kann kein Radioprogram einstellen," which means "a horse cannot tune in a radio" in German.

After the initial foreign phrase, the patter should run something like, "In a firm our size, these things will happen—people come, people go; only the receptionist is immutable. We hire the type of lawyer who has many other opportunities. Ergo, if lawyers didn't leave, it would mean that we weren't hiring the right type of people and that would be a far more serious thing than one, or a few, or several or many lawyers leaving. So, actually, lawyers leaving means that we are hiring the right type of persons, which means that the long-term prognosis for the firm is healthy. In fact, the more lawyers who leave, the healthier we probably are."

The whimsical approach is to make up a limerick for each person who leaves. Take, for example, the one about the star who left to join a small firm:

At Fairweather there was an associate
Who learned very well to negotiate.
His bargaining game
Was so good, he became
A partner in a boutique of eight.

Finally, there is the ever-popular vicious response to the associate who joins another large firm. Normally, this requires that an attack be mounted, *sub silento*, on the associate's professional ethics, sexual preferences (or lack thereof) and legal ability, while publicly wishing the associate well and taking care to point out that no ill feelings are harbored toward the little traitor.

Of course, the proper way of handling the situation will also differ depending upon to whom the explanation is being given. Variations of explanations may include:

- *To an ordinary associate* — "It is this firm's policy never to comment about departing associates." (A less polite variation of this explanation is, "None of your frigging business.")
- *To a star associate* — "Few know this, Harry, and I wouldn't want it to leave this men's room, but despite the genuflections of partners as they passed his office and the top bonuses awarded him during his three years here, X's days at FW&S were numbered. Sensing this, he snarfed up the first general partnership offer that Irkland & Kellis tossed him. In his tenuous position, who could blame him? But I thought that you, as one of our topmost associates, should know the sad truth."
- *To a partner* — Never tell a partner anything. He or she does not need to know and will gum things up by giving inappropriate explanations to other associates.

- *To a client with whom the associate worked* — Generally, a subtle allusion to Judas or to Dick Nixon is appropriate.
- *To the spouse or parent of the departed* — "We were so sorry to see him leave. Oh, what a loss we've sustained! Only the best is what we wish him."

The foregoing should make it clear, even to the most imbecilic of our partners, that handling an associate's departure is a delicate problem, best left to one experienced in such matters. Accordingly, henceforth, all inquiries regarding associates leaving should be held indefinitely by our receptionist until we can find somebody sensitive enough to whom to forward the inquiry.

Managing to Get Along

Bertha made me managing partner. Really. We had never had such a thing. But then, one day, she got a call from some legal periodical or another asking who was the managing partner, and she told them that I was. (We were in the politburo stage of management then.) Next thing I knew, there I was, listed as managing partner in a compilation of the largest 250 or 318 or something firms in the country or the world or the universe. Lucky thing for me I was on Bertha's good side that day, or Nails Nuttree might be our managing partner.

Not that Nails would not be a perfectly good managing partner. No, strike that, he wouldn't. I've thought some about what it takes to be a good managing partner and concluded that, above all, it takes somebody who is above the fray. Nails is never above the fray. Or below it, for that matter. He's smack-dab in the middle. It may be that litigators are too fray-prone to be good managing partners. I'd better add an "in general" to that one.

The managing partner has to be perceived as fair. It's not enough (or, indeed, even necessary) that he *be* fair; he's just got to be *perceived* as fair. Fairness is important in any organization, I guess, but in a law firm it's essential. Nobody knows due process like lawyers. Most of the time, in fact, they insist on an undue amount of process and rather too little substance. I guess maybe I'm perceived to be fair because I gore everybody's ox—that's what we talked about back in law school: whose ox was being gored—about equally.

Being above the fray helps a lot in achieving that perception of fairness. Frays have always amused rather than engaged me—at least the kind of frays my partners get into. I think it's healthy to let my partners fray, up to a point. Trick is to know when to call a halt and crack a few heads.

Ideally, a managing partner shouldn't even be thought to care very much about his own interests. So, people who are independently wealthy might be good candidates for the position (I hope my granddaughter Maggie doesn't read this). Myself, I've never been independently wealthy. And it would not be accurate to say that I don't care deeply about my own interests. I've always felt, though, that my own interests are pretty much best served by whatever will benefit the firm. Sounds corny, I know, but I believe it. Maybe that makes me dependently wealthy.

As I look around at many of my fellow managing partners around the country, I think that rarely has there been a clearer application of the Peter Principle—people rising to their level of incompetence. I don't mean that disrespectfully. Let me explain by relating a bit of firm history.

For many years, we, like many other firms, boasted how we were run democratically, by all of our partners. Every damn thing you could think of was put to a vote of the full partnership, from hiring a new associate to changing the design of the firm stationery. After a while, democracy gets a bit tiresome as a way to run a law firm, so we finally got beyond the democracy mystique and created a politburo.

Actually, "politburo" is one of the few things law firms didn't call those committees. Instead, they were called management committees, executive committees, policy committees, governing committees, administrative committees, planning committees and probably about two dozen other names, as well. We chose executive committee.

Of course, we preserved our great democratic tradition

through election of the members of our Executive Committee. Though our partnership agreement calls for voting weighted according to partnership percentages, in fact we used a one person, one vote system. This is because our open elections always perpetuated the incumbent Executive Committee, except for changes the incumbents thought we ought to make.

So, at the end of the day we were left with a ruling body of fifteen members (to assure representation from a broad cross-section of the firm), none of whom knew a damn thing about managing a firm. Remember, we're talking about my partners, most of whom went to law school rather than medical or business school, because they couldn't stand the sight of blood, and money seemed a bit too grubby. Our theory in creating such a large Executive Committee seemed to be that if you pooled enough ignorance, you'd be able to manage the place. Well, we did develop a rather astounding pool of ignorance. And in the process, the total time spent by this high-priced legal talent doing what they were not qualified to do became enormous and extremely expensive.

A penetrating analysis of the cost of our Executive Committee by our Finance Committee led to the suggestion that with only seven members on the Executive Committee, we could still pool enough ignorance to run the firm. As I recall, we debated the wisdom of this reduction in size for most of two partnership meetings until, at the end of the second, I announced who I thought should be on the seven-member committee.

Not too long after that, Bertha got the phone call that made me managing partner. When some of my partners read the article, they thought that having a managing partner was a pretty good idea, so we began deliberations on the wisdom of establishing that position. The argument in favor of a managing partner was pretty simple—to save the Executive Committee from doing mundane things and to make the operation run more smoothly. Great idea. But as it turned out, there were a few problems.

First, our Executive Committee didn't really want to give up power. So the functions they proposed to delegate to the managing partner were so menial that no self-respecting partner would accept the position. And even those menial functions were supposed to be subject to review by the full Executive Committee. In other words, instead of streamlining the process, what they really proposed to do was add another level.

Second problem was that, like many other firms, ours chose the most respected and productive partner to assume the position: me. At first I protested on the basis that I had no special qualifications for the position. They countered that neither did anybody else on the Executive Committee. I had to concede that.

But then I pointed out that it would be removing me from what I do best: practice law. It would be a little like taking Willie Mays at the prime of his career and saying, "Willie, I know you can hit .300 for us, make over-the-shoulder catches in clutch situations, blast thirty home runs and steal twenty-five bases, but Willie, what we'd really like you to do is run the business of the New York Giants. Now what type of financing do you think we ought to use to refurbish the Polo Grounds?" That's the first time I'd ever compared myself to Willie Mays. Old "Say Hey" Stanley. Nice ring, I like it.

Third, not only was I not particularly qualified for the position of managing partner, but I didn't *want* the damn position. And this was true, likewise, of my rainmaking compatriots at other large firms who had the greatness of managing partner thrust upon them.

In this, we rainmakers differed from the executive committee (or policy committee, or politburo) members, all of whom cherished the opportunity to serve on the committee. Let's face it—running the firm as part of an executive committee is a status symbol; it shows you are an important member of the firm. True, it takes a fair amount of time, but the tradeoff is worth it.

But being managing partner often means giving up your practice. And practicing is what us top producers like; it's what we're good at. The prestige of being recognized as the leader of the firm was certainly not worth giving up my practice. Hell, anybody who didn't recognize who was leader of this firm was dumb as cement anyway—and hadn't looked at the firm name lately.

Though this was not a concern for me, for other potential managing partners giving up their practice would be risky. What would happen if they didn't want to be managing partner anymore? Or, worse, if they did, but the firm decided they'd had enough of their management style? Picking up your practice where you'd left it would not be so easy.

Well, I *am* managing partner. So how did we work things out? Simple really. I advised the firm that I was prepared to accept the position of managing partner, but would continue to practice law. I told them that I didn't think we needed too fancy a definition of what my powers were. I had a pretty good sense of what I thought they ought to be. And if anybody thought I was exceeding my bounds, why, they ought to feel free to come in and tell me about it. I can't say that my office carpet has been worn thin by the traffic shuffling in and out to complain about how I've exercised my powers.

And we've taken some sensible steps, looking to the future. We're training some people to be managers. And they're not our top producers. We're setting fixed terms for future managing partners, and guaranteeing them some financial stability once they come back into the practice.

And we're hiring more support staff. Why, without our firm administrator, Lt. Colonel Clinton Hargraves, CPA (and all of his memos), I could never survive. In another thousand years or so, I'm confident we'll have all of this worked out. The timing should be perfect because, by then, I'll be ready to retire. Probably.

Speaking of governance, there's one more thing I've been thinking about. Over the years, I've served on my share of corporate boards of directors. And I've been impressed by the value of a breadth of perspectives in resolving issues. We law firms are mighty narrow. I wonder whether it wouldn't make sense to create a board of directors composed of our various constituencies—clients, law schools, the community, judges, employees—to help us make some of our decisions. If nothing else, establishing that kind of group would be one hell of a public relations coup. But I think there may be a lot more to it than that.

Now I know you'll tell me that there are some problems. We law firms are not publicly owned, and might not want to subject some of our information to scrutiny by outsiders. There may be issues of client confidentiality. And it may be difficult for a judge to sit on a firm's board. I'm going to let you worry about all this, if you think my idea has some merit. After all, I *am* eighty. And I've got a few more chapters to write.

Have Memo, Will Babble

Like I said, without Lt. Colonel Hargraves, CPA, our whole administrative apparatus might grind to a halt. Come to think of it, that's a thought to relish. But no, I'd never fire old Clint. I'd miss his memos too much. Here are a couple for you to savor:

To: All Personnel
From: Lt. Colonel Clinton Hargraves, CPA
Subject: Conference Room Reservations

A number of personages have expressed incomprehension regarding my memorandum of September 12 which dealt comprehensively with what I will call (for shorthand reference) the "conference room reservations problem."

My September 12 memorandum called attention to the increasing number of situations being experienced in which people are occupying conference rooms designated "Open." Now, since we are attempting to maximize the utilization factor of our conference rooms, one might think that the occupation of "open" conference rooms would be something that I and others interested in increasing that utilization factor would applaud. And so we would, except for one important fact—"Open" conference rooms are usually not open. This has humiliated many of our attorneys and clients who have happened upon some pretty tawdry scenes. The unopenness of our "Open" conference rooms is most frequently attributable to the time gap between the instance of creation of the reservation designating use (or non-use) of a conference room and the date for which the conference room is to be used (or non-used, as the case may be), which may sometimes approximate three months.

I am pleased to report that the Executive Committee, with my assistance, has formulated a plan for attacking this gruesome situation by reducing (and, we hope, eventually eradicating) this time warp. I am also pleased to announce that we have enlisted the able support of Sally Raftelianco to help with our warping problem (or "de-warping opportunity," as I prefer to think of it). Unfortunately, this will necessitate removing Sally from the Wang-implementation function which I announced last week that she would assume in lieu of her word-processing and secretarial functions, which have been ably assumed by Ronnie Green and Lucinda Densely, for which I and the rest of the firm would like to express our appreciation. Erin Rock will temporarily assume Sally's Wang-activating duties and I am sure you all join me in wishing her good luck in this important new position.

In the interim, the E.C. has authorized me to announce the following procedures for conference room utilization. Due to the high occupancy of "Open" conference rooms, commencing immediately, nobody shall occupy those rooms. Due to the high cancellation rate for reserved conference rooms, however, anybody may occupy a conference room reserved for another. Persons reserving a conference room and actually wanting to use one may call the Reservationist on the day of intended use and the Reservationist will assign such persons "Open" conference rooms, on a last-in, first-out basis.

We recognize that this temporary solution is not perfect and that some will be inconvenienced until implementation of whatever new scheme Sally may come up with. However, in the spirit of cooperation for which this firm may justifiably be proud, I am confident that we shall survive this crisis. Remember:

Conference rooms are at a premium and the problem is continuing, or we wouldn't write a memo like this.

And here's Clint's memo announcing his own arrival at the firm:

To: All Personnel
Copies To: All Personnel
From: Lt. Colonel Clinton L. Hargraves, CPA
Subject: New Director of Administration

I am pleased to tell you that effective immediately we have successfully concluded the hiring function involved in procuring a new Director of Administration for our Firm. I know that you will want to join in extending a warm Fairweather welcome to our new Director of Administration, Lt. Colonel Clinton Hargraves, CPA.

Clint (I feel I can call him that since I've know him since birth) comes to us from Adour Henderson & Co. where he arrived after matriculating as a jargon major from an undergraduate institution of high renown. His outstanding background places him in a tremendous position to eradicate some of the problems that make it impossible for the Firm to realize its fullest and highest potentiality.

Clint's initial function will be to assemble a top-flight administrative staff, then to reassemble that staff and then to juggle and again reassemble that staff so that it may be designed to effectuate the goal of maximizing efficiency and effectiveness. And, if necessary, reassemble the staff yet again. Clearly, this is important.

To the extent possible, the implementation of this goal will be realized by promoting and upgrading people from within to new roles since this will help to assist in the morale function and will make available to our existing personnel fine career-building opportunities to achieve their highest potentiality. Of course, promoting and upgrading from within will also mean demoting and downgrading from within which will adversely impact the morale building function. In this regard, Clint will try for a minimalization of demoralization occurrences by announcing demotions as changes in function and asking that everybody congratulate the demoted staff person. Please play along with this, clearly.

Clint will keep all of our "top-notch" personnel painfully abreast of every administrative move with semi-daily memoranda delineating all functional adjustments so that they will be not only the finest team in the city, but also the best-informed. Clearly, this is important.

Clint will be facing a significant challenge in achieving the major objective of reassessing our complex, multifaceted organizational approaches so as to make them more responsive to the requirements of our professional team. While we have the nucleus of a fine administrative team, only through the implementation of key task forces and the proliferation of managerial and supervisory personnel can we enhance the responsivity of our administrative apparatus to our short run and long term goals. Clearly, this is necessary.

Clint will bring a high degree of motivational ability that should permit him to make a fine contribution to matters ranging from establishing and implementing consistently administered policies and procedures to eradicating the elongated turn-around time problem in word processing.

Clearly, solutions to our problems—and Clint prefers to think of them not as problems, but resolution opportunities—will not come over-nocturnally. Our primary task will be to articulate goals that will help us work the "kinks" out so that our fine Firm will run again like a well-greased machine, but always with individual attention to the little nuts and bolts who comprise it.

We welcome Clint!

Retire Early, Avoid the Rush

I don't have lunch with my law school classmates much anymore. A big group of them are dead, and don't return phone calls. And most of the others are mandatorily retired.

I don't shy away from saying that my classmates are dead. I've never cottoned much to "passing on" or "passing away" or being "no longer with us." (Sounds too much like "letting associates go.") We all know what it means, why not say it. I'm in no particular rush to join that great law firm in the sky, but, hell, when the time comes, my briefcase is packed and my time sheets are up to date.

And speaking of not returning phone calls, being dead's about the only excuse I can think of for not returning them. You might say I'm a bit fanatical about that. It stems from an experience I had as a young lawyer that I've never forgotten.

I represented a fellow named Jason Fairton, who owned what was then a rather sizeable wire products factory on the west side of town. I'd handled his corporate matters for several years, and we'd become friends. At the time, I was engaged in contract negotiations in which Jason's corporation was to acquire one of its principal suppliers, Avco Wire Corporation. Jason was what you might call a demanding or, if you were less generous, a difficult client. He wanted attention to his matters, and he was not the tiniest bit bashful about asking for it.

About mid-morning one day, Bertha handed me a message to call Jason "right away." The "right away" was superfluous; Jason always wanted to be called right away. I was running out to a meeting at the time and had several other appointments scheduled for the rest of the day. I knew that Jason was calling to check on the status of the Avco contract, and I had nothing new to report.

When I returned to the office, early afternoon, I had another message to call Jason right away, "it's important." "Important" was Jason's way of announcing that this was his second call. On my desk was a draft of a contract that I'd promised another client I'd get out, and I had another meeting in half an hour, so I ignored Jason's second message.

Next call I got from Jason was that evening, at home. He asked me to meet him at James Falsworthy's office at ten the next morning. That puzzled me. Falsworthy was a partner at another firm. He was not involved in the Avco matter. I asked what the meeting was about, but Jason would say only that I would find out tomorrow.

The next morning, when I was ushered into Falsworthy's office, Jason was already there. "Stanley," he said, "I want you to meet my lawyer, Jim Falsworthy. Please send your files over to him."

After I picked up my teeth, I managed to mumble out the semblance of a question the gist of which was "Why?"

Jason said, "Jim here says that he returns phone calls."

"But I was in the middle of three things," I said. "And I had nothing new to report on Avco. I was going to get back to you today."

"You don't know what I was calling about, Stanley. It might have been an emergency; maybe my kid was locked up at the police station."

"But you would have said if it was an emergency," I argued.

"Maybe I would have, and maybe I wouldn't. But I'm the client, Stanley, and I'd like to decide when I need to talk to you. Since that evidently is not acceptable to you,

I've found somebody who doesn't find that notion so objectionable."

I wanted to punch that so-and-so in the nose, right there. Fortunately, I didn't, because the SOB would probably have pressed battery charges. Turns out, though, he did me a favor, taught me an important lesson.

It took me almost five years to get Jason's business back. He never would tell me whether anything important was up the day I didn't call him back. Told me that was covered by the attorney-client privilege—him and Falsworthy. Stubborn old cuss, Fairton was. That's probably why we got along so well in his later years, before he retired and handed the business over to his sons.

Mandatory retirement, that's what I was going to talk about. Me, I've been retired, mandatorily, for ten years now. At least that's what the partnership agreement says. And partnership agreements don't lie. Or do they?

When I was forty or fifty, I sometimes thought I might like to retire. Right then. I thought maybe I'd open a fancy French restaurant. I'd be the pastry chef. But for me, that was always a passing fancy.

And the older I've gotten, the less attractive retirement seems. I'm not sure why. Maybe it's that when you're younger, there appear to be so many options, post retirement. Market's a tad thin these days, though, for eighty-year-old lawyers who are used to running the whole show.

Our firm debated for some time whether to put a mandatory retirement age into our partnership agreement. (Of course, come to think of it, there are very few things we did not debate for *some* time—chief among them, the things we debated for a *very long* time.) Proponents of a mandatory retirement age pointed out that it would mean we wouldn't have to decide when to tell one of our senior partners that he would have to retire. That argument leaves me cold. I guess it would be nice if we didn't have to make any tough decisions. But we do. And I don't think we do ourselves much of a favor by trying to duck or postpone those decisions.

In any case, I'm grateful that my partners have seen fit to let me continue to practice. Turns out I've had some of the most productive years of my career subsequent to my mandatory retirement. But, like most everything, I wouldn't be surprised to see the whole focus of mandatory retirement change soon.

For one thing, it may not even be an issue. After all, it becomes an issue only if lawyers want to stay on beyond whatever age is retirement age. (I leave aside here, without comment, another class of retirees—those partners who retire from practice but don't tell anybody and continue to pull down their partnership draw.) While my contemporaries tend to want to hang around—die with our boots on—I don't see that desire in my younger partners. Many of them would like to be out of here today, if they could. For them, the idea of retirement's no passing fancy, either. They got into this business when it was supposed to be a genteel sport, like baseball used to be. But the rules changed on them almost as soon as they suited up. Doesn't look like there'll be an instant replay anytime soon. And with the big takes some partners pulled down in the 80s, more of them may actually be in a financial position to retire.

At the same time, there may be a lot less incentive for the firm to keep us older lawyers on board. Used to be, we oldtimers were valuable because of the client relationships we'd established. But those were the good old days— you know, when a client was a client forever. With the deterioration of client relationships that I've spoken of earlier, though, we codgers are a whole lot less valuable.

But even if we *are* going to continue with mandatory retirement, I'm not sure we've pegged the age at the right level. Seems to me, we ought to be thinking of a mandatory retirement age in the neighborhood of, say, fifty. With the pace that lawyers keep today, they burn out pretty quickly. Pretty soon, finding an older lawyer is going to be as rare as finding an old investment banker.

Yes, the pace of the law has gotten a bit out of hand. Of course, the telephone has made demands on people ever since Mr. Bell first said, "Mr. Watson, come here, I want you." But at least Mr. Watson was not reachable by car phone, by beeper and portable phone, on airplanes and by fax. At times, this excessive reachability must make all of us wish for retirement, at least in one sense of the word—a place of seclusion or privacy. (Listen to me, first expounding on the need to return phone calls immediately, and then decrying the existence of phones altogether. Oh well, as they say, consistency is the hobgoblin of small minds.)

But retirement at fifty has its drawbacks. Seems a darn shame to waste all of those years of experience. Maybe firms should constitute their senior partners a council of elders and tap their experience and advice on the problems the firm faces. I know plenty of senior partners who would be happy to serve in that capacity for a whole lot less money than they're making now. A little respect would more than compensate for the difference. After all, that's what many of us went into the practice looking for in the first place.

Il Partnershipio

Sometimes I think that the process of making partner is too dramatic for real life and should, instead, take place in the form of an opera—perhaps, "Il Partnershipio." Here then (with apologies to anyone—opera lover, person of Italian ancestry or woebegone associate—who I may unintentionally offend) is the way I envision such an opera might enfold.

ACT I

The curtain rises on a conference room in the offices of the prestigious Bologna law firm of Sephugia, Sephugia and Goldstein. Arturo, an associate who has been with the firm for over five years and specializes in real estate law, is seated at a conference table piled high with documents. Also at the table are six other people.

Dressed in a four-piece suit (two vests), Arturo moves to the front left of the stage and, cupping his hand and putting it to his mouth to signal to the audience that he is speaking to them and cannot be heard by the others in the room, sings the famous introductory aria, "O Mio Rusumeo," in which he immodestly boasts of the background that led to his hiring by the firm. After rattling off virtually all of his accomplishments since the crib, including his Italian Jurisprudence Award in contractos and his many mooto courto triumphs, he finally returns to the conference table.

In the ensuing septet, the people around the table each identify themselves and sing of what has brought them to the conference table. Unfortunately, since all of them are singing at once, nobody in the audience can make out a word. Everybody in the audience, however, is presumed to have read the libretto and to know that they are attending an important condominium closing in which Arturo is representing the builder and condo developer Roderigo del Seisin, who, unbeknownst to Arturo, is planning to use the property that he is purchasing for whorehouse condos, the first of their kind in Bologna.

The seller, an old widow by the name of Maria Malalucca (whose husband, Real Lee Malalucca, left the property to her when he died from lemon gelatos that had been poisoned by the grandniece of the evil zoning administrator, Rodrigo dello Fixitto), thinks that the property is a worthless swamp, notwithstanding its location in downtown Bologna. She has been driven slightly daft by her nogood son, Hank, who, despite being valedictorian of his college class, has never aspired to be anything other than a toll collector in the exact-change lane of the autostrada. Maria spends the first act spraying the conference room to rid it of the malaria that she thinks has been brought in from her swamp property by a buzzle of flies. She sings her famous aria "Agli Uffizzi non vogliamo tsetse" ("No Tsetse in the Uffizzi") while continually squirting a can of Raid.

Also at the table is Stefano Sephugia, the eighty-three-year-old senior partner in Sephugia, Sephugia and Goldstein, Arturo's law firm. As we learn from his "Io son il secondo Sephugia" ("I Am the Second Sephugia"), Stefano is not the originator of the firm, but succeeded to the position of senior partner upon the death of his older brother Alfredo, who died when a wound, accidentally inflicted by a notary public in affixing his stamp to a document, became infected. Stefano spends each day in this conference room and participates in whatever meetings are being held there. He falls asleep from time to time, but wakes up abruptly and says, "Well, I guess that's alright," every five minutes or so.

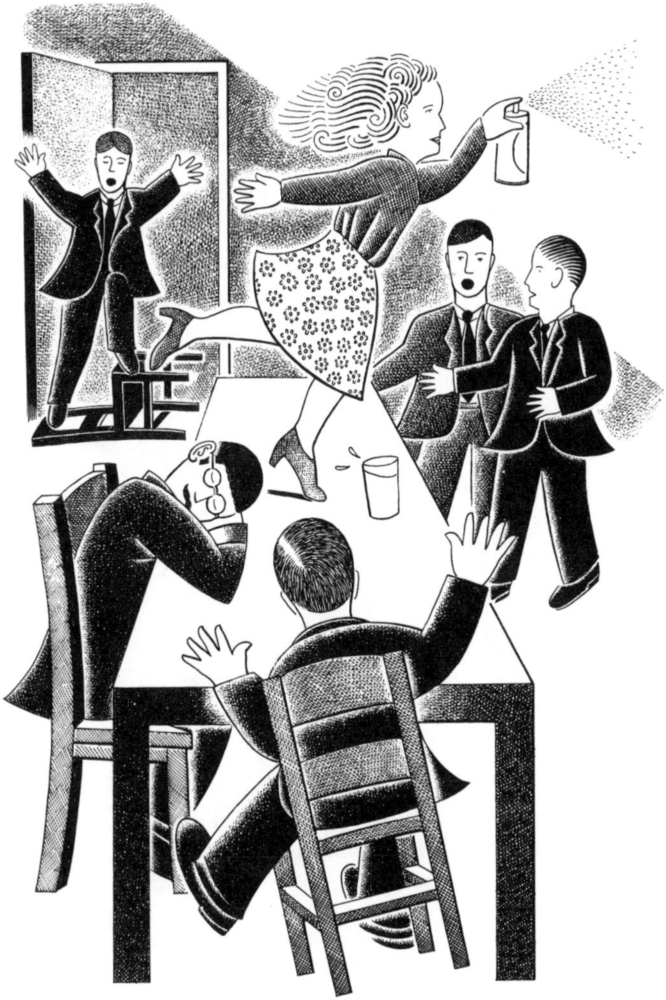

The other two people in the room are Rosa and Rocco Petrocelli, brother and sister paralegals. They sing their enchanting duet "Oh siamo solo un paio di paralegali" ("Oh We're Just a Pair of Paralegals"), in which they bemoan the life of a paralegal and shuffle all of the papers on the table back and forth, putting them in different piles, then returning them to their original piles.

Arturo gets up from the conference table and again goes to the front left of the stage, cups his hand and sings to the audience of his anxiety over the forthcoming decision about whether he will be made a partner in the firm: "Perdio se non mi fanno socio faccio" ("If I Don't Make Partner, I'm Gonna Have a Fit"). And the curtain falls as the others (except Stefano, who is asleep) run over to where Arturo is standing and sing the angry quintet, "Se non di cantare dove non ti si può ascoltare" ("If You Don't Stop Singing Where We Can't Hear You, We're Gonna Give You a Crack on the Head").

ACT II

The scene is in the same conference room four days later. Stefano Sephugia is asleep in the same chair that he occupied in the first act. Seated around the table with Stefano are five other people all wearing anywhere from three- to six-piece suits, except one, who is wearing a swimsuit and scuba gear.

Lucca Provolone, who is chairing the meeting, announces in his aria, "Arturo sì o Arturo no" ("Arturo, Up or Down with Him?") that the next order of business is consideration of whether Arturo should become a partner in the firm. The others around the table all sing at once the quintet "Arturo socio? Giammai!" ("If He's a Partner, We're All Guppies"). During the quintet, Stefano falls asleep, but awakens at the end and announces, "Well, I guess that's alright."

Lucca quiets the Executive Committee with "Zitti, sitti vi tolgo i proventi" ("Quiet, Quiet or I'll Cut Your Partnership Share") and asks each of them to express his view separately. One of the partners opines that the partnership cannot afford to make another partner: "Che scherzi son questi?" ("Is This a Joke? We're All Broke"), while another says that he does not believe that Arturo has achieved the requisite level for partnership: "Divino ancor non è" ("He's Not a God Yet"). The fellow in the scuba gear realizes that he has come to the wrong place, "Pesce non c'e; corallo hemmeno" ("There Are No Fish, There Is No Coral"), and announces his intention to leave just as soon as he votes on the partnership question. Stefano awakens and says, "Well, I guess that's alright".

Just then a tremendous commotion is heard out in the hall and one of the partners rushes in to the meeting to announce that Channel 69 Eyewitness News has sent a crew to the firm, which is in the process of interviewing Arturo in his office. The curtain rings down as the Executive Committee sings its famous sextet "Su partiam, su partiam, Arturo alla tele andiamo a guardar" ("Let's Adjourn and Watch Arturo on the Tele").

ACT III

The scene is in Arturo's office, where a cameraman and Channel 69's Lolita Bellissima are setting up for the interview. We learn from Lolita's lilting "Il piano di Roderigo è all'aria" ("Roderigo's Plan Is Dead") that Arturo has discovered that Roderigo was intending to turn the property purchased from Maria into whorehouse condos and sell them on a one-hour timesharing basis. In keeping with the new Code of Professional Responsibility, Arturo has run to the police and ratted on his client.

Just then the telephone rings, Arturo puts his hand over the receiver and tells Lolita that it is Maria who has called to thank him: "E il fazzo con e Raid" ("It's the Nut with the Raid"). Maria suggests that Arturo put Maria on the speaker phone so that all of the viewing audience can hear her first-hand, but Arturo explains that he cannot do that: "Son solo un umile associato senzo l'interfon" ("I'm Only a Lowly Associate Without a Speaker Phone"). Lolita is shocked to hear this and asks Arturo when he will become a partner and, in his touching aria, "Solo in cielo un socio sarò" ("Maybe Only in Heaven Will I a Partner Become"), he explains to her that there is no guarantee, even after his long years of service, that he will be made a partner on this earth.

At this point, several of the Executive Committee members, who had been listening to the interview from outside of Arturo's office and who sense that the possibility of Arturo's not becoming a partner is creating adverse publicity, sing the poignant trio "Oh desdetta socio si ha da far" ("Oh Shit, We'd Better Make Him a Partner Now") and burst in to the interview to congratulate Arturo on becoming a partner. Stefano, who has fallen asleep on the floor outside of Arturo's office, sits bolt upright and says, "Well, I guess that's alright," and the entire cast, in a gala finale, sing and dance to "Ma sì che va bene" ("Well, We Guess That's Alright").

Crisis

I think I'm having a midlife crisis. Don't laugh, some of us are late bloomers. Think about all of those fellas in the Bible. They must have had midlife crises in their hundreds. Hell, I'll bet eighty would have been downright precocious for a midlife crisis, back then.

I think the whole concept of crisis may be anachronistic. Webster says that crisis is "an unstable or crucial time or state of affairs whose outcome will make a decisive difference for better or worse." Seems like we're up against that most every day, doesn't it.

Now that I think about it, we lawyers wallow in crisis; it's our clay, the stuff with which we work. On the one hand, we're called on to avert crises. By carefully negotiating and drafting a contract, I can avoid a collision down the road. On the other hand, we have the capacity to create a crisis—by bringing a lawsuit, or by taking an intransigent position in a negotiation. And (on the third and fourth hands, I guess) frequently we are hired to assess whether a crisis in fact exists and to respond to genuine crises.

But anyway, I was talking about *my* crisis, midlife or otherwise. And it's this: I've been made a very attractive offer. Really. No, it's not from another large law firm; hell, none of them would have me. And it's not from the Chicago Cubs; though, heaven knows, they could use my baseball savvy in the dugout. It's not from some fancy French restaurant, either, wanting me to replace their chef.

No, my offer comes from a real close friend of mine—Maggie. Actually, she made it quite some time ago. I thought she was just joking, at first. But she wasn't.

Her offer was this—to join her at legal aid. She's moving to Chicago to head up the office here. She says that they have plenty of litigators, but they need to beef up their business expertise. So she offered me the post of head of the business law department, reporting directly to her—at almost thirty-five grand a year. Not peanuts.

Now, I protested, of course. First off, it smelled of nepotism to me, and I told her so. She told me that was nonsense. She said she'd conducted a thorough search, and I'd turned up as the most qualified candidate. She couldn't help it, she said, if I happened to be her grandpa. Got to grant her that one, I suppose.

I told her I had gotten pretty used to running my own show, though, and didn't think I would do very well as part of an organization that I didn't control. She promised to give me considerable leeway in running my department, at least until I fouled things up and forced her to step in.

I protested that I was accustomed to dealing with major transactions involving large amounts of money and very complicated legal issues. I didn't know whether I could handle legal-aid-type problems. She wondered whether that meant I could only serve rich people and thought that poor people weren't really people. She's pretty good at getting my goat.

Well, I've thought about this offer long and hard (the way we lawyers are taught to think about everything), and have come to the following conclusion—why not. Of course, I couldn't just pick up and leave the firm. That would be too rash and, after all, I *am* still a lawyer. Fortunately, though, I still swing a little bit of weight with our pro bono committee. So, when I suggested the firm might want to loan an attorney to legal aid for a year as part of our pro bono effort, they thought that was a splendid idea. They asked whether I had anyone in mind. I told them I'd noodle it over a little and get back to them.

So I guess this is my formal announcement—oyez, oyez, oyez—I'll be taking a year off. Bertha's coming with, of course. She says that she needs a change, too. And we're

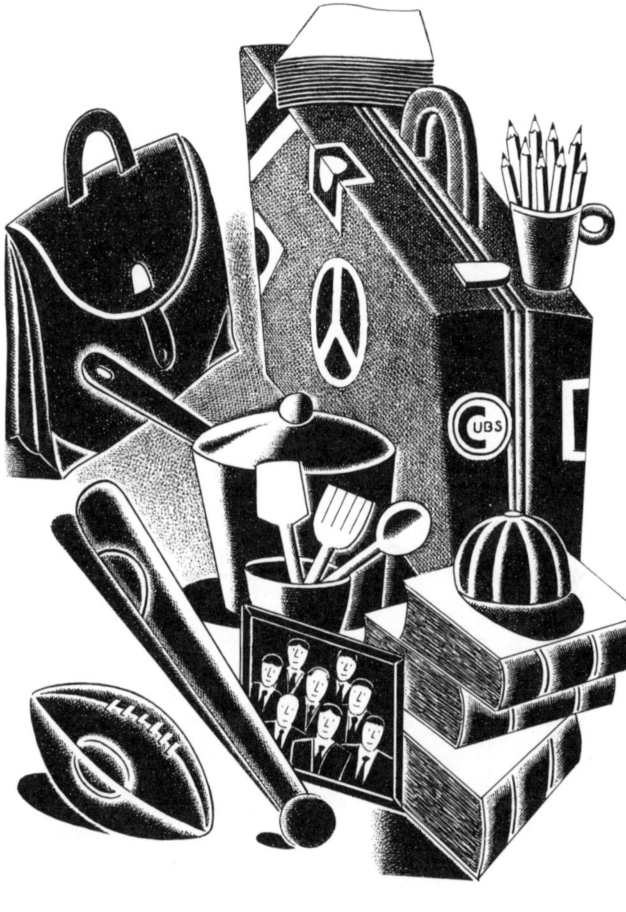
CUBS

a package deal, Bertha and me; sort of a latter-day Koufax and Drysdale deal. Bertha's Koufax.

Wish I could have finished this book for you, before I leave, but Maggie says she needs me right away. And she doesn't expect I'll have much spare time to write in the next year, either. So I don't have much choice. I sure don't want to start off on the wrong foot with my new boss.

I've got to go pack up a few things now, before I take off. Truth is, I haven't been this excited about something in quite a while. If I'm not mistaken, it was T. S. Eliot who said that old men ought to be explorers . . . Ponce de Fairweather. Nice ring to it, don't you think?

Until Death Do Us Part—Or Longer

Here's the latest version of the partnership agreement according to which I've been mandatorily retired for ten years now. It's a perfect example of the kind of work lawyers can come up with when they represent themselves.

Agreement made this 24th day of December, 1992, and effective *nunc pro tunc* as of the beginning of time, by and among the "Corner Partners" and certain others too insignificant to list (hereinafter known as "Others" and occasionally as "Partners" when the Corner Partners are feeling expansive).

Whereas some of the parties hereto have been practicing a modicum of law of late; and

Whereas, other parties hereto have been flicking legal advice off the tops of their heads for years; and

Whereas, just about everybody wants something in writing; and

Whereas nobody can find a copy of the old partnership agreement, which has got to be around here someplace.

Now therefore, the parties will settle for the following:

ARTICLE I
OFFICES

Certain of the Partners are Corner Partners. Life is unfair.

ARTICLE II
PERCENTAGES

2.1 The partnership percentage of each Partner shall be the number of points of such Partner, determined by the following recipe, divided by the total number of points of all Partners so determined;

a. Take the square root of the dollars billed and collected by that Partner, minus three times the dollars billed but uncollected in the last twelve months;

b. Add to this the number of hours logged by the Partner, minus twice the number of hours logged on pro bono matters, divided by 189;

c. Add the number of years with the firm minus two times the number of years with the firm in excess of 35;

d. Add the number of the partner's close friends in the firm who have partnership percentages in excess of 2.33 less twice the number of close friends with partnership percentages under 1.87; and

e. Season to Stanley's taste.

2.2 Any Partner who emerges with more than 4 percent is hereafter sometimes known as a "Big Hitter" and shall be entitled to one Associate at his beck and call for each quarter of a percentage point in excess of four. "Associate" shall mean any person who, with the fullness of time and the ripeness of old age, may have the ability or dumb luck to become an Other.

2.3 In case of disputes regarding partnership percentages, the principle "to each according to his needs" shall apply. Big Hitters shall determine needs. All Partners acknowledge that Big Hitters have big needs.

2.4 In no event shall the total partnership percentage exceed 100. Notwithstanding the foregoing, whenever total percentages exceed 100, those Others who volunteer shall have their percentages reduced. Any Other selected by the Big Hitters shall be deemed to have volunteered.

ARTICLE III
BILLING

3.1 All Partners shall bill at least the required rate, unless a member of the Billing Committee approves a lower rate. The Billing Committee shall be composed, from time to time, of the five meanest, toughest sons of bitches in the firm. The required rate shall mean that rate per lawyer which, when multiplied by the number of hours worked, will permit the Corner Partners to live at the RLAF ("Required Level of Affluence").

3.2 Partners are urged to bill the recommended rate. The recommended rate shall mean whatever the computer (after checking other firms' rates) thinks can be passed off to clients without significant risk of discipline from the Bar Association Disciplinary Commission. Anything above that is gravy.

3.3 The above billing rates need not be adhered to for Cherished Clients. "Cherished Client" means any client of a member of the Big Hitter All-Star Committee, as referred to in Article XI hereof.

ARTICLE IV
PARTNERSHIP PROFITS AND LOSSES

4.1 Corner Partners and Others acknowledge and confirm that partnership profits are a big secret and must not be disclosed, either to Associates or to the IRS. Anybody who tells is subject to the loss of his Corner or an Associate at his beck and call, and may be subject to increased federal income taxation.

4.2 Losses shall be apportioned among Associates.

ARTICLE V
HIRING COMMITTEE

The Hiring Committee shall be composed of the six least accessible Partners during any hiring season. Hiring season shall run from Labor Day until the third day of Chanukah. No person shall hire without a hiring license, which shall be issued by the Game Warden, who shall be selected by the Big Hitters All-Star Committee.

ARTICLE VI
ASSOCIATE SALARIES

Associates shall be paid the going rate. The going rate shall mean the minimum salary that Associates will accept without going.

ARTICLE VII
USE OF ASSOCIATES

Those Partners without Associates at their beck and call must request Associates from the Headhunters Committee, which oversees the painfully slow development of Associates. Those Associates who have survived three or more years at the firm or 2,000 cups of the firm's coffee (whichever comes first) shall be deemed to have entered the Free Fire Zone. All Associates in the Free Fire Zone may be used by any Partner, provided such Associate is properly trapped by a Partner. An Associate may be trapped in any office or common area of the firm. Bathrooms shall be deemed sanctuaries.

ARTICLE VIII
BLAME AND CREDIT

Partners do not make mistakes. Blame for anything that goes wrong with respect to a particular file shall be allocated to the Associate whose initials are the last on the file. Credit shall continue to be distributed, in accordance with accepted firm practice, on the principle of LRP (Least Responsible Partner).

ARTICLE IX
PARTNERSHIP MEETINGS

9.1 Meetings of the full partnership shall be held every once in a while, or less frequently if possible.

9.2 The purposes of partnership meetings shall be to permit Others to blow off steam and to permit the Big Hitters All-Star Committee to pontificate on matters of its choice.

ARTICLE X
VOTING

All Corner Partners and Others shall have one vote on all matters which properly come before the partnership. The Big Hitters All-Star Committee shall determine what matters properly come before the partnership.

ARTICLE XI
ALL-STAR COMMITTEE

The Big Hitters All-Star Committee shall be composed of those Partners having the five largest partnership percentages and one additional Partner who is friendliest with those five and not unacceptable to any of them. The Big Hitters All-Star Committee shall have the power to make such decisions as it may, from time to time, damn well want to. The Committee shall, every now and then, submit matters to the full partnership for their uh-huh.

ARTICLE XII
RESIGNATION OF PARTNERS

12.1 Any Partner may resign by tendering his or her written resignation to the Big Hitters All-Star Committee. Each Partner hereby irrevocably appoints the Big Hitters All-Star Committee as his or her agent and attorney-in-fact for purposes of tendering resignations. All resignations shall be deemed voluntary and submitted for personal reasons, so far as the press is concerned.

12.2 A resigning Partner shall be entitled to zip.

ARTICLE XIII
BLANK

This article is intentionally left blank.

ARTICLE XIV
RETIREMENT

Retirement shall be mandatory at the age of 70. Notwithstanding the foregoing, retirement shall not be mandatory at the age of 70.

ARTICLE XV
FIRM NAME

The firm name initially shall continue to be Fairweather, Winters & Sommers. Upon the death, bankruptcy, insanity or retirement (tee hee) of any of the above, other than Stanley J. Fairweather, his name shall be exorcised and no new name shall be added until such time as the firm name is reduced to "Fairweather &."

ARTICLE XVI
GOVERNING LAW

The law of the jungle shall apply.

ARTICLE XVII
AMENDMENT

This Agreement may not be amended. Notwithstanding the foregoing, this Agreement may be amended at any time on the whims of those Big Hitters who are Chosen People. They know who they are.

ARTICLE XVIII
TERMINATION

The Agreement shall terminate on the first to occur of the following:

a. The First of Ayar, 6928;
b. The coming of the Messiah;
c. The Resurrection;
d. The Twelfth of Never;
e. None of the above.

In the event of an occurrence described by section (b) or (c) above, this Agreement shall be superseded by the Word of God; provided, however, that if God shall turn out to be a Corner Partner, this agreement shall continue in full force and effect.

HUMOR FROM CATBIRD PRESS

For Lawyers and Other Denizens of the Legal World

The Handbook of Law Firm Mismanagement. Also by Arnold B. Kanter. The misadventures of a mythical law firm, told via its memos and notes of committee meetings. "To the law firm experience what M*A*S*H was to the Korean conflict." —*Chicago Bar Assoc. Record.* Our bestseller. $12.95 paper, 192 pp.

Trials and Tribulations: Appealing Legal Humor. Edited by Daniel R. White, author of *The Official Lawyer's Handbook*. A collection of the best in legal humor by humorists such as Twain, Benchley, and Perelman, as well as legal humorists such as Prosser, Arnold, and Mortimer. With lots of cartoons. A great gift. $19.95 cloth, 320 pp.

For Travelers — Armchair and Otherwise

The Humorists' Guide Series. Edited by Robert Wechsler. Collections of stories, memoirs, descriptions, light verse, and cartoons all about traveling abroad. Thurber, Dickens, Buchwald, Blount, and all the rest. From irony to nonsense and back again, these volumes contain all the absurdities and delights of travel. "A first-rate gift for the traveler-to-be as well as for stay-at-homes." —*New York Times.* Each volume is $10.95 paper, 200 pp.

In a Fog: The Humorists' Guide to **England**
Savoir Rire: The Humorists' Guide to **France**
When in Rome: The Humorists' Guide to **Italy**
Here We Are: The Humorists' Guide to the **United States**
All in the Same Boat: The Humorists' Guide to the **Ocean Cruise**

These books can be found or ordered at better bookstores everywhere, or they can be ordered directly from Catbird Press. Just send a check for the appropriate amount, plus $3.00 shipping no matter how many books you order, to Catbird Press, 16 Windsor Road, North Haven, CT 06473. For information or a complete catalog, call 203-230-2391.